DAVID O. MCKAY LIBRARY

3 1404 00798 2488

P9-DTR-676

IMPROVING
TEST SCORES

FEB 27 2006

WITHDRAWN

MAY 0 6 2024

DAVID O. McKAY LIBRARY
BYU-IDAHO

IMPROVING TEST SCORES

A Practical Approach for Teachers and Administrators

SCOTT MANDEL

Zephyr Press

Chicago

Library of Congress Cataloging-in-Publication Data

Mandel, Scott M.
  Improving test scores : a practical approach for teachers and
administrators / Scott Mandel.
    p. cm.
  Includes index.
  ISBN 1-56976-202-3
  1. Test-taking skills—Study and teaching.   2. Educational tests and
measurements. I. Title.
  LB3060.57.M36 2006
  371.26′071—dc22

                                                                    2005009408

All rights reserved. The purchase of this book entitles the individual teacher to
reproduce the forms for use in the classroom. The reproduction of any part for an
entire school or school system or for commercial use is strictly prohibited. No
form of this work may be reproduced, transmitted, or recorded without written
permission from the publisher.

Cover and interior design: Rattray Design

© 2006 by Scott Mandel
All rights reserved
Published by Zephyr Press
An imprint of Chicago Review Press, Incorporated
814 North Franklin Street
Chicago, Illinois 60610
ISBN 1-56976-202-3
Printed in the United States of America
5   4   3   2   1

This book is dedicated to the faculty and staff of Pacoima Middle School in Los Angeles. This exceptional group of educators has tirelessly worked toward, and succeeded at, raising the test scores of their students in an economically depressed immigrant area. Their efforts offer an example of how teachers in our society today can work toward giving all students opportunities for an excellent education.

Contents

Acknowledgments

The production of any book involves the work of many people. First of all, I want to thank the wonderful people at Zephyr Press and its parent company, Chicago Review Press. Working with them has always been an absolute pleasure! I want to thank my editor, Lisa Reardon, for her brilliant job with my words, and Jerry Pohlen, senior editor, for his assistance in formulating the ideas for this book. I also want to thank Scott Rattray for his beautiful design work on the cover and the interior.

A number of excellent educators in the Los Angeles Unified School District lent their invaluable feedback, ideas, and suggestions to these pages. These people reviewed the material from a variety of different perspectives in the attempt to make this book as valuable as possible to all teachers and administrators. They are, in alphabetical order, Katie Andrews, Linda Azzarella, Melodie Bitter, Jana Davenport, Michael Fishler, Robert Krell, Kathie Marshall, Mercy Momary, Linda Phillips, and Robert Schuck.

I want to especially thank the following people for their specialized contributions to this work: Katie Andrews and Kathie Marshall, for their expertise with the English language; Melodie Bitter, for her work on the special-education portions of the book; and Dr. Robert Schuck, for his expert advice on and ideas for the critical thinking section.

A number of excellent ideas were submitted for this book through both conversations and written correspondence. Many are listed and credited in "A Treasure Chest of Teacher Tips" (page 103); others are sprinkled throughout the three remaining sections of the book. Thanks to the following for sharing this material: Carolyn Akin-Meyers, Geri Byrne, Edward Contreras, Jana Davenport, Vickie Decker, Patrick DeVuono, Stephanie Flores, Tom Giles, Jeanette Hernandez, Kurt Krueger, Lana Lanayan, Elizabeth Morones, Jane Orr, Linda Phillips, Sue Prieto, Robert Schuck, Aida Tatiossian, Mary Whiteley, and Linda Wright.

Introduction

> *Another faculty meeting. More handouts displaying our school's standardized test scores. More frustration. Scores from the last test are compared to those of the previous year, compared to those of other schools in the district, compared to those of other schools in the state. Scores broken down by students' races, ethnicities, and means of paying for lunch. The principal reprimands us . . . .*
>
> *"Our scores didn't go up enough last year. . . . We're still in the same percentile . . . . We need to improve even more this year, and every teacher is going to be expected to buckle down and teach only to the standards that are tested so our kids do better on the exam . . . . For the rest of the afternoon, I want you to get into your departments and figure out how you're going to improve your students' test scores."*
>
> *It's the same speech the principal gives every year when our test scores are published in the local newspaper. Now they're going to expect me to give up teaching more of my curriculum to concentrate on The Test. Why don't they just give me the actual test, and I'll teach that material?*
>
> *There has to be a solution.*
>
> —thoughts of thousands of anonymous teachers in America today

Education Today and the Primacy of Testing

The story told above unfortunately captures the current reality of teaching and testing in schools around the country. Federal and state governments demand that our students' knowledge be assessed using standardized tests that may or may not directly match teachers' classroom curricula or suit students' personal abilities. Schools are not evaluated on their overall educational program or learning environment; nor are they evaluated on their students' holistic development.[1] They are evaluated solely by a numerical standard that is derived via standardized

---

[1]For an example of a holistic evaluation that assesses an entire educational program—see Eisner 1994.

tests—tests that may or may not be suited to the various learning styles of students. The emphasis is on whether or not students have acquired a predetermined body of knowledge, not on the process of learning. This is reality today.

The problem with this mind-set is that it flies directly in the face of what businesses expect from our high school graduates today. They want employees who can function both independently and collaboratively, who can work well with others and who view themselves as part of an overall organization (see Carnevale 1991, 1996, 2002). If new workers need specific knowledge, companies arrange for intensive workshops or classes to provide that knowledge.

Unfortunately, businesses have become increasingly aware that, due to the education system's stress on standardized tests and on students' acquisition of a set body of knowledge in order to pass those tests, students now enter the workforce unable to function in the cooperative working environment that businesses want to promote[2] (Wayne *et al* 1992; Barker *et al* 1998).

This is in direct contrast to federal and state governments that impose severe penalties on schools whose students do not meet a certain standard based on this standardized testing. As a result, school superintendents (whose job security is often largely based on their districts' performance) put pressure on their administrative staff (whose job security is often largely based on their schools' performance), who put pressure on school principals (whose job security is often largely based on their schools' performance), who ultimately must put pressure on the teachers. Testing has become a system of "accountability of all." Job security is a strong motivating factor for both teachers and school administrators, and they are forced to "play the game" even if they do not believe in it. This is today's reality. And standardized testing is not going to go away any time in the foreseeable future.

We all must learn how to live with it whether we like it or not. So what are we going to do?

The Skewing of Test Scores

Refer to the opening anecdote concerning the frustrated teacher. She and her colleagues at that school worked diligently to improve their students' scores, and they succeeded in raising scores from the previous year's level. However, the school remained in the same percentile in relation to other schools taking the test. This, more than any other aspect of standardized testing, has led to the frustration of

---

[2]For a detailed example of the teaching methodology and classroom environment that best prepares students for success in today's business world, see Mandel 2003b.

both teachers and administrators alike. And it's a matter of simple statistics: if everyone in the district or the state also succeeds in raising their students' scores, then everyone goes up—*and your scores stay in the same place (percentile) as they were, in relation to everyone else.* For example, imagine that your school was in the twenty-fifth percentile and that you raised your scores by 100 points. If every other school in the district did about the same, your school would remain in the twenty-fifth percentile, even though you demonstrated significant improvement.

The result of this system is this: when a school's quality is judged on its *percentile*, or rank compared to other schools, the school is not being judged on how well it has improved the educational progress of its students. Instead, it is being judged on whether it has improved *more* than other schools. This is a situation that needs to be changed.

A Teacher's Dichotomy

Teachers are educated and certified professionals. All have acquired a BA, and the majority have either acquired or completed many hours toward acquiring a master's degree. A number of classroom teachers have doctorates. There are thousands of National Board Certified Teachers in this country who have demonstrated commendable teaching skills. Just like other certified professionals, certified teachers have demonstrated their expertise regarding a specific body of knowledge in their field, and they know how to do their jobs. As is the case of workers in all professions, there are some teachers who are inadequate and who should be removed from the classroom; but, as is also the case of workers in all professions, the vast majority are competent and qualified to provide their students an acceptable, if not exemplary, education. They know how to teach, and they know what to teach based on their given curricula.

Unfortunately, the testing craze of today has led to teachers being told not only what to teach, but also, in a frightening number of instances, *how* to teach. An increasing number of schools are adopting prescribed programs that outline every step teachers are to take, every lesson they are to teach, and, in many instances, the exact words they are supposed to say. And often the decisions about adopting these programs are made by people who have not been in a classroom in years, if ever.

Hence, the teachers' dichotomy: figuring out the balance between (a) what they believe should be taught and how they believe it should be taught (based on their professional expertise) and (b) what is being directed, in terms of both subject matter and method of teaching (based on orders from "above").

This is a dichotomy that teachers need to deal with while doing an underpaid job that most of their critics would never dream of undertaking.

The Purpose of This Book

This book is meant to demonstrate to teachers how they can raise their students' test scores while keeping the integrity of their teaching skills and expertise. It is derived from practical ideas generated by observations of, and conversations with, numerous classroom teachers of all levels and subject areas.

The key is that the material in this book is practical—it is meant to fit into the realm of what really can be accomplished in the individual classroom and throughout the school. Ideas such as "change the date of the test to June" or "have teachers design the test to better fit the curriculum"—although excellent ideas—are not included in this text. They simply aren't practical, and they will never happen. Instead, the book focuses on what teachers *can* do within the normal, everyday classroom. It offers workable ideas on adaptations that can be made to the prescribed curriculum, to the school environment, and to teaching methods—adaptations that can raise test scores while maintaining the integrity of teaching.

How to Use This Book

Each section is divided into specific topics with easy-to-follow subsections:

- Grades: the grade levels to which each issue is most applicable (not every issue is relevant to every grade)
- Time Line: a time line for addressing each issue during the year
- The Issue: the basic issue addressed in the subsection
- The Idea: a workable suggestion on how to address the issue (Note: this section is not titled "Solutions," for there are no absolute solutions. All ideas need to be adapted to your particular situation, and your individual teaching style.)
- Concluding Thoughts: a summary of the major points presented

As you read this book, remember that every teacher is different; every teacher is unique. The ideas presented here must be stylized, adapted, and molded into a solution that works for you. The ideas are generalized; the emphasis is on the underlying, transferable philosophies that each idea presents. As a result, this book suits every teacher's individual situation.

Make the material in this book work for your individual teaching environment. It's your classroom, and your life, for almost seven hours a day, five days a week—regardless of what standardized tests your students are required to experience.

1

Teacher Issues

Ms. Conteh sat in the faculty meeting and listened as the principal once again reviewed the school's standardized test scores. Was this the fourth or fifth time he had done so this semester? The endless review of this data was boring, depressing, and utterly frustrating. The school's scores had risen every year for the past eight years, but they never seemed to be good enough. Ms. Conteh and her fellow teachers had worked incredibly hard to raise the scores—and obviously they were succeeding—but their efforts appeared to be not enough to satisfy the administration, which showed little appreciation for the teachers' efforts.

At this moment, Ms. Conteh's morale was as low as it could be. The faculty members at her school were doing everything they could. They were stymied as to what else they could do.

- How could they ensure that their classroom curricula covered the material that would be tested, while still maintaining their independence as teachers?
- How could they ensure that they covered the curricular material that was addressed on the standardized tests if their classroom textbooks weren't adequate?
- How could they improve their students' critical thinking skills to help them do better on the tests?
- How could they improve their students' study and testing skills to help them do better on the tests?
- How could they keep up their own morale during testing so that it wouldn't affect their students?

As Ms. Conteh sat there reviewing the test score charts again, she wondered how much longer she would continue to teach. Was it worth it anymore?

Matching the Curriculum to the Test and to Your Teaching

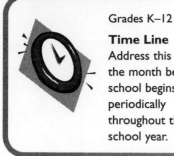

Grades K–12

Time Line
Address this issue the month before school begins and periodically throughout the school year.

The Issue

How can I ensure that my classroom curricula cover the material that will be tested, while maintaining my teaching independence?

The Idea

Too often what is taught in the classroom does not cover what materializes on end-of-the-year standardized tests. Regardless of good intentions, excellent teaching skills, and adherence to the prescribed standards, if the eighth-grade history section of the standardized test contains material from the seventh- and sixth-grade curricula, it is doubtful that you will have had the time to cover those areas within your allotted class time for the year.

Sometimes teachers have a measure of control over adaptations to their curricula; sometimes they do not. A growing number of districts are implementing district pacing plans, benchmark exams, and even prescribed, scripted programs that limit teachers' flexibility in determining the classroom curricula.

The growing classroom dilemma that teachers face today is determining how to cover all of the material that will be tested or that is required by the district, maintaining both an element of independence in their teaching and the ability to capitalize on their personal expertise, which has been gleaned through years of study and experience. In other words, how can you teach what you know and believe should be taught while making sure that you cover everything that is required to be taught?

Advance Planning

The primary goal of advance planning is to ensure that you both cover the topics that will be tested on the exam and meet district, school, and personal curricular requirements. Most standardized testing takes place during the ninth month of school, even though some subjects and material addressed in the tests are taught after this time. Combine this with the imposition of district pacing plans, benchmark assessments, and prescribed programs and the results are often teacher frustration and, ultimately, lower test scores. However, advance planning, although time consuming, can alleviate much of this problem. Three ways of completing this complicated task are to develop your own personal pacing plan, to prioritize concepts and standards, and to integrate material whenever possible. Before attempting any of these strategies, you will need a list of all the topics and concepts covered on the final standardized exam. Your administration should have this information.

◎ **Develop a Personal Pacing Plan.** Using a calendar and the list of the material covered on the test, create a time line for the school year, mapping out the curriculum by the approximate number of weeks necessary to cover the topics to be tested. Please note that this plan is only a guideline. Some material may end up taking less time than was allotted; some may take more. The key is to ensure that all necessary areas are covered before the test.

A personal pacing plan keeps you focused on what needs to be completed and ensures that everything necessary is covered. The following is an example of such a plan. This time line is taken from a sixth-grade English class.

Month	September				October			
Week	1	2	3	4	1	2	3	4
Topic	Intro to Literature/ Opening of Year		Fiction: Plot		Fiction: Character			

Month	November				December			
Week	1	2	3	4	1	2	3	4
Topic	Grammar: Parts of Speech		Fiction: Setting		Fiction: Theme		Vacation	

Month	January				February			
Week	1	2	3	4	1	2	3	4
Topic	Nonfiction Forms: Biographies, Autobiographies, Memoirs, Articles, Etc.				(2nd Semester) Poetry			

Month	March				April			
Week	1	2	3	4	1	2	3	4
Topic	Poetry	Grammar: Phrases, Sentences, Clauses		Vacation	Drama			

Month	May				June			
Week	1	2	3	4	1	2	3	4
Topic	Standardized Testing		Novels				End-of-Year Business; Vacation	

Creative writing is taught throughout each unit in relation to that subject area.

Remember, this is only a guideline. Units can be expanded or contracted as need arises. The key is to ensure that all necessary areas are covered prior to the standardized test.

◎ **Prioritize Concepts and Standards.** One major impediment to raising test scores is that the tests simply cover more than you can practically teach during the entire school year—much less during the eight and a half months you have before the testing weeks. Therefore, it is necessary to prioritize the concepts and standards that you will cover within your classroom curricula.

The key to this task is to determine which areas are more heavily emphasized on the exam. Today's standardized tests usually provide guidelines that indicate the weight given each topic (your administration should have this information). In order to effectively prioritize curricula, this information is critical. For example, let's say that the grammar portion of the test contains the following distribution of questions:

35%	sentence structure
10%	clauses
25%	parts of speech
20%	punctuation
10%	phrases

After completing your personal pacing plan, you discovered that, based on everything you are required to teach in order to prepare for the test, you have only six weeks available to spend on grammar. Given this limitation, you can prioritize and decide how much time to devote to each of these five aspects of grammar during those six weeks.

Prioritize the above list of topics based on their relative weights on the exam by marking each one with an A, B, or C:

A = must be taught to mastery level
B = students must be exposed to; teach to mastery level
   if time allows
C = expose students to only if time allows

Going through the list, you might label the five areas as follows:

A	35%	sentence structure
C	10%	clauses

A   25%   parts of speech
B   20%   punctuation
C   10%   phrases

Based on your prioritization and personal pacing plan, you will know to spend four to five of the six weeks on sentence structure and parts of speech. A week or two may be devoted to punctuation, and you will cover clauses and phrases if time allows.

The concept behind this is that it is better to have students master the most important parts of the test rather than to simply expose them to everything and hope they learn it well enough to correctly answer the questions.

Here is a graphic representation of probable scores using this method. For argument's sake, assume that by simply being taught everything "as usual" in the limited time allotted, students will correctly answer 50 percent of the test's questions. By teaching the material with more emphasis than usual, but not to mastery, teachers can expect that students will get 75 percent correct. Through teaching to mastery, teachers might expect students will answer 90 percent of the questions correctly. For a test that is comprised of one hundred questions, the following results would be expected:

Subject Area	Number of Questions	Number of Questions Answered Correctly by Teaching Everything in Time Allotted	Number of Questions Answered Correctly by Prioritizing the Concepts (A, B, C)
Sentence structure	35	18	32
Clauses	10	5	2*
Parts of speech	25	12	22
Punctuation	20	10	15
Phrases	10	5	2*
Total correct	100	50	73

*Number correct based on random guessing percentages (one in five chances to guess correct answer). To improve students' abilities to guess correct answers, see "Teaching Study and Testing Skills" (page 34).

As you can see, by prioritizing the concepts and standards you will teach, and by teaching the most important ones (rather than trying to expose students to every topic in the time allotted), student scores will be significantly higher.

Integrating Material Whenever Possible

Probably the easiest way to make additional time to cover the necessary material is to integrate various material and concepts whenever possible. This can be accomplished in two basic ways—by integrating material within a subject area and by integrating material across subject areas.

◎ **Integrating Material Within a Subject Are**a. After looking at all of the concepts and material that will be covered on the test, you can frequently pinpoint subjects that can be integrated together and taught within one unit, rather than teaching them as separate units.

For example, in English classes, grammar can be integrated with comprehension writing assignments. The concept of using figurative language can be taught within a poetry unit and then extended to your prose units.

In history class, the skill of reading graphs can be taught during any unit that contains material that can easily be graphed. For example, when discussing how differences in the populations of slaves and citizens in Athens and Sparta had a direct bearing on those cities' economies, you can teach pie charts.

Related math concepts can often be combined. Fractions, percentages, and ratios have many similar components that can be taught together.

◎ **Integrating Material Across Subject Areas**. Very often material can be integrated between different, but related, subject areas. This is especially the case with English and history and with math and science. Skill or concept areas that are common to both subjects can be divided among them. Although this is most easily accomplished when the same teacher teaches both subjects, it can also be accomplished when two or more teachers are involved. The only requirements are the time and desire to work together to divide and integrate these areas.

For example, both English and history teachers often assign research papers. This time-consuming but important skill can be combined so that students write one paper instead of two—the history teacher teaches and grades for content, and the English teacher teaches and grades for mechanics and expression. If the Civil War is part of the history curriculum, the English teacher might use a novel about the Civil War as part of the "novel reading" unit. If Shakespeare is taught in English class, the political climate of Shakespeare's day might be covered in history class. All of these integrations free up significant time to cover other required material.

There are many skill areas that math and science teachers both teach. Statistical analysis, graphing techniques, and metric measurement are common in each curriculum. Teachers can divide the teaching of these common concepts so that they are not necessarily taught twice to students. Again, this will greatly alleviate teaching time constraints.

Teacher Tool

Using Homework to Cover Material

Homework is an excellent tool to use to cover material you can't address within the time allotted during class. The following excerpt is taken from the book *The New-Teacher Toolbox*:

Too many teachers believe homework to be nothing more than a review of the day's teaching. I disagree. If students can do ten division problems correctly in class, doing ten more at home is not going to further their abilities. The half-hour to an hour that they would spend on those problems, however, can be equivalent to an extra class period for covering additional curricular material.

Homework should be used not only for review, but to practice new concepts and introduce new curricula. When the material is introduced in class, and students understand the task assigned, homework can be used, just as class time is, for basic practice on important curricular material. Larger assignments can be assigned and spread over two or three days (thereby also giving students the opportunity to learn and practice time management skills). For instance, if a history chapter is divided into four sections with questions, instead of doing all of them in class, cover three in class and assign one for homework over a couple of days. You will automatically cut class time on this chapter by 25 percent. All of the material—both from homework and class work—can be graded as you would grade any other curricular assignment.

You need to be aware of not giving too much to do (every class and age can handle varying workloads), and to allow for those students who have comprehension problems. Still, rather than giving busywork for homework, you can use the time to help cover curriculum that you cannot get to in class.

Mandel 2003a, pp. 34–35

This integration of material across subject areas not only saves teaching time, but also leads to better understanding of the curricula by students, who now can see the interrelationship of concepts and areas across disciplines.

District Pacing Plans and Benchmark Assessments

An increasing number of districts are incorporating pacing plans and benchmark assessments in order to ensure that their teachers are following the curriculum and covering all of the standards that will be tested at the end of the year.

A district pacing plan is a mandated plan that instructs the teacher to teach a set amount of material over a specific period of time. It may be general in nature, such as giving a list of standards to be covered in a ten-week period. Or it may be specific, directing the teacher on what to teach every single day of a reporting period.

Benchmark assessments are "mini" standardized tests that are given to determine if students are on the correct track in terms of learning all that will be contained in the end-of-year standardized test. These tests are given at specific "benchmarks" throughout the school year—usually at every reporting period, or at eight- to ten-week intervals. Benchmark assessments usually are directly connected with district pacing plans.

There are a number of major problems with the implementation of district pacing plans and benchmark assessments. First, these plans and tests are often created by out-of-classroom personnel, some of whom have not taught in a classroom in many years. They have lost touch with the reality of today's students and school environment. Second, pacing plans assume that students understand the concepts in the allotted time frame. They leave no time for remediation or for expansion of concepts. Third, teachers often have limited, if any, input into the process. As a result, what and when teachers are directed to teach is often not what and when they believe should be taught. Finally, 180 teaching days (the normal school year) are seriously reduced by a variety of interruptions such as shortened days, assemblies, safety drills, etc. These are not considered in the pacing plan.

Here is a true story. A middle school English teacher in a large metropolitan district created the following personal pacing plan for the year:

> *First Semester:*
> Sixteen weeks: prose (plot, character, setting, and theme for
>   both fiction and nonfiction)
> Four weeks: grammar (parts of speech)

Second Semester:
Ten weeks: poetry (including elements of figurative language)
Two weeks: grammar (phrases and clauses)
Eight weeks—drama

In her plan, the year was divided into specific blocks that built on each other, and all major parts of literature were covered. Creative writing and comprehension skills were built into each unit, matching the core subject matter. Unfortunately, the district instituted benchmark assessments every ten weeks, as well as a pacing plan to match those tests. The district pacing plan looked like this:

First Semester:
First ten weeks: narrative
Second ten weeks: exposition

Second Semester:
First ten weeks: response to literature
Second ten weeks: persuasion
(aspects such as plot, character, etc., were included and
    repeated throughout the four different sections)

Not only did the new directive have no discernable logical progressions between the four areas, but, completely to her dismay, the teacher discovered that the district pacing plan included almost no material on poetry and drama (elements of each were merely scattered throughout the curriculum).

Unfortunately, this is the situation in which many teachers now find themselves. The district plans obviously could not be ignored; neither, however, could the teacher's valuable teaching expertise developed over the course of a career in the classroom. The dilemma, therefore, is to figure out how to use the district-mandated pacing plans, do well on the benchmark assessments, and still maintain one's personal credibility as a teacher. In other words, how can you teach what is mandated to be taught and, at the same time, teach what you believe *should* be taught?

The following are some suggestions on dealing with this dilemma. The three basic types of scenarios are presented: a general pacing plan without benchmark assessments; a general pacing plan with benchmark assessments; and a specific pacing plan with benchmark assessments.

◎ **General Pacing Plan Without Benchmark Assessments**. This is the easiest scenario in which to teach. You have general guidelines or areas to cover in each semester's or marking period's curriculum, but there are no benchmark assessments. In this scenario, you should match what the district wants you to teach with your personal pacing plan (see above). Any areas mandated that are not covered in your personal plan should then be added in the most appropriate spot within the curriculum. It is important you ensure the coverage of all mandated aspects of the district pacing plan. The difference is that you have the freedom to determine the most appropriate place to teach the material, based on your own personal plan.

◎ **General Pacing Plan with Benchmark Assessments**. This is the most common form of district pacing plan now in use. In this scenario, the district provides guidelines to use in teaching over a period of time (usually eight to ten weeks), then gives an assessment based on those guidelines. In this situation, you need to first follow the district pacing plan exactly to see how it works. You are looking for two specific pieces of information: first, how much time does the plan actually take? (Plans often include less direction than is required to fill the entire testing period span.) Second, how much duplication is there in the district plan? (In other words, how much leeway is there to combine or remove elements while still covering all required standards?) Once these two pieces of information have been determined, you can then add to or adapt the district pacing plan to your own personal plan in a balancing act that covers both the district's requirements and your own.

Consider the above situation regarding the middle school English teacher as an example of this procedure. After implementing the mandated district plan exactly as it was stated one year, she discovered that she could cover all of the required material in six weeks. That allowed her four weeks of each testing period to focus on the areas that were not covered in the district plan—in her case, poetry and drama (she integrated her prose curriculum throughout the district's four components). Now her classroom curriculum looked like this:

First Semester:
Four weeks: introduction to prose
Six weeks: district pacing plan 1 (narrative) followed by bench-
    mark assessment

Four weeks: poetry (part one)

Six weeks: district pacing plan 2 (exposition) followed by
    benchmark assessment

Second Semester:

Four weeks: poetry (part two)

Six weeks: district pacing plan 3 (response to literature)
    followed by benchmark assessment

Four weeks: drama

Six weeks: district pacing plan 4 (persuasion) followed by
    benchmark assessment

◎ **Specific Plan with Benchmark Assessments.** In this scenario, there are
    significant limits to any teaching freedom or determination of curriculum
    by the teacher. Every day's or week's curricula are basically structured and
    subsequently tested. In this situation, all you can do is integrate material
    whenever possible (see section on integration above) and use homework to
    cover material you cannot cover in class, or to teach various aspects of the
    district pacing plan material (see Teacher Tool Box earlier in this chapter).
    With a specific district pacing plan, you will need to use some creativity if
    you want to figure out ways to bring in areas that you feel should be taught.

Prescribed/Scripted Programs

Prescribed/scripted programs basically lay out every step of the lesson for the
teacher. Many of them go so far as to instruct the teacher on to what to say. These
programs are most prevalent in elementary school–level reading, but they are also
being developed for the middle school.

Unfortunately, an increasing number of districts have begun to use these
plans. Increases in scores are often demonstrated in the first few years of implementation; however, due to numerous factors, scores often *decrease* after the
third or fourth year (see Pogrow 2001 and Jones *et al.* 1997). Another problem
with prescribed/scripted programs is that there is virtually no teacher input
regarding curricular issues or time allotment, often leading to the detriment of
other subjects. There are many elementary schools that spend so much time
adhering to the programs that they have virtually eliminated social studies, science, and the arts from their students' curricula.

If you have a prescribed/scripted program in your classroom, there is little
that you can do to manipulate your classroom curricula. However, there are two

steps that you can take in the process of finding levels of adaptation. Be aware that the amount of adaptation allowed is often at the discretion of the administrator in charge of your program.

◎ **Follow the program first before you adapt it**. It is critical that you spend your first year with the program following it as directed without adaptations. By doing so, you will know the program well enough that you can analyze its components and subsequently adapt it to your needs.

◎ **Prioritize the concepts and other aspects of the program**. Go through the program and make note of all of the concepts you are directed to teach. These should then be prioritized into three areas (similar to the section on prioritizing concepts and standards above). Each one is subsequently marked with an A, B, or C:

> A = must be taught/implemented
> B = should be taught/implemented if time allows
> C = expose students to only if time allows

By doing this, you can look at your classroom holistically and find a balance among the requirements of the program, the areas you feel are necessary for students to learn, and the requirements of the overall classroom curricula.

Concluding Thoughts

A common problem teachers face is simultaneously ensuring that classroom curricula cover the material that will be tested while maintaining their teaching independence. Advance planning is critical when dealing with this situation. Teachers need to develop personal pacing plans, and they must prioritize concepts and standards to be taught. It also helps to integrate curricular material whenever possible, both within a subject area and across subject areas. This is especially important when the teacher is required to implement district pacing plans, benchmark assessments, and prescribed programs.

Teaching with the Curricular Materials You're Given

Grades K–12

Time Line
Address this issue throughout the school year when you are planning your units.

The Issue

How can I ensure that I cover the curricular material found on the standardized tests even if my classroom textbooks are inadequate?

The Idea

Textbook publishers and standardized test makers are ordinarily separate entities. If either your textbook or the standardized test is national in design, then there is a strong probability that what is on the test will not be completely covered by the textbook. This problem is not as severe in states in which the publisher and the test maker produce state-specific editions of their products; in those cases, the test and the textbook are each created in accordance with specific state standards.

When both test and text adhere to the state's standards, you do not have to worry as much about not having the required curricular material at your disposal. In this scenario, the text is in line with the standards, which are subsequently aligned with the test. Everything you would need is included in the textbook. In this scenario, the major concern is whether or not your textbook covers the subject matter adequately. You must determine whether or not the book contains enough practice material to lead to student mastery of the subject matter. If it does not, you will need to find or produce supplementary material.

This section is written primarily for those teachers in states where there is *not* a state-specific, standards-aligned test and/or textbook. Keep in mind, however, that even teachers in states that do use state-specific materials must be aware of changes in state standards and their school's place within the textbook adoption cycle. Most textbook publishers produce new editions for state adoption every seven years (there is some variation depending on the state). Changes to the annual standardized tests are more frequent. If the educational standards in your state are changed, adjusted, or supplemented within the time period between textbook adoptions, you may find yourself with a textbook that is no longer aligned with either your state's new standards or the final state exams. If you find yourself in that situation, then the ideas presented in this section may become more relevant.

First determine which of these three categories applies to your school:

- You have state-specific standardized tests and texts, both of which are current and aligned with state standards.

- You have state-specific standardized tests and texts aligned to state standards. However, you are awaiting a new textbook adoption to match changes in the state standards

- You have either nationally based standardized tests or texts, at least one of which is not directly aligned to state standards.

In the cases of the second and third scenarios, it falls upon the teacher to locate and teach curricular material that is tested but not covered in the textbook.

Advance Analysis

An advance analysis, although rather time-consuming, will make your curricular planning and subsequent teaching more productive and efficient. Compare the subject matter that is covered on the test to the subject matter that is included in your textbook. Most state standardized tests include materials that list the concept areas and/or percentages of items covered for each grade level. (If that information is not produced by your testing company/entity, then you and your fellow grade level/subject area teachers need to analyze the tests personally during the following testing cycle to determine conflicts between what is tested and what is covered in your texts).

Teacher Tool

Using Bulletin Boards for Curricular Material

You can expose students to information and concepts that are included on the test but are inadequately addressed or are missing from textbooks through the use of curricular bulletin boards. You can post material that covers the necessary areas, and students can read the material in their spare time. (You can give them a question or two to ensure that they spend time looking at the boards.) These boards can also be used as centers that students must visit during their center time.

For instance, using the example of personification discussed on page 15, you might post any number of fun excerpts of Shel Silverstein's poetry, along with questions about the examples of personification that are used throughout the poem.

The same thing can be done with all tested subject matter that is inadequately covered, or not covered at all, in the class textbook.

◎ **Analyzing the test and the text.** Once you have compiled a list of the areas and concepts that are covered on your particular standardized test, you should search through the beginning pages of your teacher's edition of the textbook and determine where each concept is addressed. Most of today's textbooks have this listed, selection by selection, either in the introductory pages of the book or at the start of each unit.

Here is an example of a chart that is easy to construct. The material is derived from the "poetry analysis" section of an upper-grade elementary school standardized test:

Poetry Concepts Covered on Test	Textbook Pages on Which Concepts Are Taught
Poetic structure (stanza, verse)	35–38, 87–88, 145
Metaphor	39–40
Simile	40–41, 276
Personification	Not covered in this text
Author's purpose	35–36, 88, 137, 145, 275, 303, 335

As the chart makes clear, the vast majority of the poetry concepts covered on the test are addressed at some point within the textbook. However, after completing this analysis, there are two problems that immediately become apparent for this English teacher:

- Personification is addressed in the test, but it is not covered in the textbook.
- The text may not include enough material on metaphors to allow students to master the concept on the test.

Once this analysis is completed, you can now plan to supplement any deficiencies found in a textbook.

◎ **Adjusting Your Curriculum Planning to the Analysis.** In "Advance Planning" (page 2), you learned how to create a personal pacing plan that encompasses all tested areas. After completing the test and textbook analysis mentioned above, you should compare your analyses to your personal pacing plan and decide how to rectify any deficiencies that are found.

Using the example above, you may have already planned to teach personification using materials and methodologies from sources other than the textbook. However, if you basically follow your text, personification may not be included within your plan. Since this is an area tested, you now need to both add it to the curriculum at some point and locate materials outside of your textbook with which to teach it.

Unfortunately, in today's economy, supplemental curricular budgets have been severely slashed. You should not be expected to lay out the money (without reimbursement) to make up for the deficiencies of a classroom textbook. Luckily, there is someplace you can turn—a place that contains virtually everything any teacher might require, all at no cost. That place is the Internet.

Using the Internet to Supplement Curricular Material

The Internet has become the ultimate teacher's resource center. The curricular material available online is seemingly endless. More important, a school in a lower socioeconomic area has as much access to this material as does one in a higher socioeconomic area.

Please note, this discussion of incorporation of the Internet does not pertain to student use within the school day. That is an entirely different issue. Rather, this discussion concerns *teacher* use, primarily at home or wherever you do the majority of your curricular planning.

The primary problem teachers have with incorporating the Internet into their planning is a personal lack of digital literacy (Gilster 1997). Teachers normally have literacy in their primary subject areas. A math teacher can be given a new math textbook and instinctively know how to use it in the classroom. An English teacher can be handed a new novel to introduce to students and immediately know where to look for supplemental materials. An American history teacher can be assigned to a world history class and teach successfully because that teacher has literacy in the teaching of history.

Digital literacy involves the use and integration of curricular material found online. It involves three primary components:

- You instinctively know what is "out there," whether or not it is available online
- You know how to quickly and efficiently locate material on the Internet
- You know how to effectively integrate this material into the curriculum

For example, you know that both the eighth- and eleventh-grade standardized history tests ask questions about the role of Thomas Paine's *Common Sense* in the

American Revolution. Unfortunately, your history textbook does not include a copy of the document, and to order it somewhere will take a couple of weeks and some unreimbursed expenses. However, if you had digital literacy you would know:

◎ that the document surely exists online, as virtually every important historical document is now available somewhere on the Internet

◎ that, although you may not know the address of a site that contains the information you are seeking, that site can be found by consulting a general education Web site, which can quickly lead you to the right place

◎ how to use the document in a classroom discussion on author motivation and reader reaction.

The first aspect of digital literacy (knowing what is online) comes from experience. The last aspect is a natural result of teaching literacy. It is to the second aspect—knowing how to quickly and efficiently locate the material—that the discussion now turns.

◎ **General Education Web Sites.** A general education Web site is one that contains links to other educational sites. The linked sites have already been analyzed and categorized. More important, you know that they are safe, educational, and usable. In effect, general education Web sites are educational portals—places that you go to first to locate information online when you do not already know a specific web address. Think of them as online Yellow Pages for teachers.

Nowadays there are numerous online sites that contain listings of other great sites for teachers. However, two specific sites have been around for about a decade, and they are considered the original general educational Web sites:

Kathy Schrock's Guide for Educators
    (http://school.discovery.com/schrockguide)
Teachers Helping Teachers (www.pacificnet.net/~mandel)

Whereas Kathy Schrock's Guide for Educators is an excellent educational site that lists hundreds of the best online educational resources, the Educational Resources page of Teachers Helping Teachers is a bit easier to use. There are fewer categories and site listings to scroll through, which lessens search time. The site is also more discriminating in its listing of Web sites. Three specific criteria must be met in order to be listed on Teachers Helping Teachers, each of which is designed to help teachers locate good educational material quickly and efficiently. An included site must:

- be general in nature—there are no "Civil War" sites, but there are general history sites that include numerous, more specific subtopics;
- include hundreds of links to other sites, thereby allowing you to access the specific information needed; and
- be a nonprofit entity. Sites created by universities, nonprofit organizations, and individuals tend to include fewer links to for-profit entities and sites that require a payment or the purchase of something in order to get curricular materials.

Using the example of Thomas Paine's *Common Sense*, you would do the following to obtain a copy of the document via the Teachers Helping Teachers Web site:

1. Go to the Educational Resources Page of Teachers Helping Teachers.
2. Scroll down to the History/Social Studies Resources Online section.
3. Scan for pertinent sites listed in this section. Pinpoint a listing for a site titled The Historical Text Archive.
4. Click on the link to this site.
5. Follow the trail to your document: click on Links, then on United States, then on Revolution, then on Thomas Payne, Common Sense.
6. Print the document and make copies for students.

This entire process takes less than one minute using a standard dial-up connection.

By listing these general education Web sites as bookmarks or favorites on your browser, you can immediately locate excellent free educational material to supplement your textbook's inadequate or missing material.

◎ **Comprehensive Subject Matter Web Sites.** Comprehensive subject matter Web sites operate in much the same way as do general education Web sites, except that these sites are subject specific. Of the numerous Internet sites of this nature, some of the best ones in the four major tested subject areas are:

English
Children's Literature Web Guide
www.ucalgary.ca/~dkbrown/index.html

Math
The Math Forum
http://mathforum.org

Social Studies
History/Social Studies for K–12 Teachers
http://home.comcast.net/%7Edboals1/boals.html

Science
Cody's Science Education Zone
http://dc.ousd.k12.ca.us/~acody

Each of these Internet sites contains links to hundreds of additional sites that focus on specific categories within the subject. By simply following one link to another, you can quickly and efficiently access virtually any curricular material you need. Like the general education Web sites, the site that covers your particular teaching area(s) should be saved as a bookmark on your browser, to be referred to on a continual basis.

Here are a couple of examples that illustrate how the material from these comprehensive subject matter Web sites can be incorporated directly into your curricula:

An English teacher discovers that the concept of personification in poetry is included on the test, but is not found in the literature textbook. The teacher knows that many poets regularly use personification in their work, but few examples are at her disposal at home (where she is planning next week's lessons), and none of those are appropriate for elementary school students. The teacher decides to look online for examples of personification in poetry that are appropriate for her students in order to put together a lesson on personification. This is how easy it is to locate and use this core material:

1. Go to the Teachers Helping Teachers Educational Resources Page and scroll down to the Language Arts Resources Online section.
2. Click on the link to Children's Literature Web Guide.
3. Follow the path to the desired material by clicking on Stories on the Web, then on Songs and Poetry, then on Poetry for Kids. This page provides numerous Internet sites that are brimming with age-appropriate poetry that exemplifies personification. Read through a few of poems and select two or three that use personification.

4. Copy the poems and paste them to a word processing document. Add your own questions for discussion (e.g., "Find the examples of personification"; "How are the animals showing human behavior or using human emotions?")

5. Print and copy the page for student use.

Teacher Tool

Why Using a Search Engine May Not Be a Good Idea

When looking for Internet sites, the first temptation is to use a search engine such as Google. Whereas this works for finding most resources online, it can be problematic when you are looking for good educational material.

The problem with search engines is that they locate *everything* that is found online in a subject area. For example, a search for "personification" on Google resulted in 185,000 listings. Of those, the top ten included sites that offer college-level definitions, three sites that didn't work, a couple of links to for-profit companies that sell English-oriented materials, and a couple of lesson plans that incorporated the concept of personification—none of which was appropriate for elementary school students.

The strength of the Internet is not in its ability to locate ready-made lessons, but in its ability to locate materials that you can use in your own lessons. By keeping this in mind when locating supplemental material online, you can ensure that your lessons are specifically designed for both your students and your particular teaching style. Although you can often find usable sites through a search engine, the most efficient way to acquire this material is to go through educational Web sites such as the ones described in this chapter.

Another benefit of using educational Web sites rather than a search engine is that you discover sites you may not have otherwise known about. For example, the teacher who searched for Thomas Paine's *Common Sense* discovered links to not only the *Historical Text Archive*, but also to *The Food Timeline* and *American Memory*, as well as to numerous interesting materials on the American Revolutionary War that could be integrated into her curriculum. The process is similar to going to purchase something at an educational book store—you invariably leave with materials you originally had no intention of buying.

A math teacher determines that his textbook doesn't cover the concept of probability well enough. He wants to locate some additional problems for students to use for individual practice. The following procedure shows how easy it is to locate supplemental material online:

1. Go to the Teachers Helping Teachers Educational Resources Page and scroll down to the math section.
2. Click on the link to The Math Forum.
3. Follow the path to the desired material by clicking on Math Resources by Subject, then on Prob/Stat, then on Classroom materials for teachers and students, then on "Problems and Puzzles." The page offers numerous probability-related activities that can be printed and used in the classroom to supplement the material found in the class's textbook.

Through the use of online resources, you can locate and subsequently cover material that is tested but is either inadequately addressed or nonexistent in your classroom textbook.

Concluding Thoughts

Sometimes you find yourself in a situation where items that are covered on the final standardized exam are not addressed in your textbook. This is frequently the case when tests and/or textbooks are not state-specific and are not aligned with state standards. In this situation it is important to analyze the material on the test and in the textbook in order to discover areas that may be inadequately addressed, or completely missing from, your textbook. Once these areas are discovered, you can plan to teach them within your personal pacing plan. The Internet can serve as the ultimate teacher's resource center and provide this material. Provided you acquire digital literacy, both general education Web sites and comprehensive subject matter Web sites can quickly and efficiently lead you to excellent free curricular material.

Teaching Critical Thinking

Grades 4–12

Time Line
Address this issue throughout the school year, especially during the first couple of months of school and the month before the final standardized tests are given.

The Issue

How can I improve my students' critical thinking skills so that they can do better on tests?

The Idea

The history department was baffled. On the final standardized test were questions that pertained to the previous two years' curricula—material that was not revisited during the current school year. In addition, questions were asked about historical facts that were either not discussed in the textbook or that were mentioned in a superficial manner. Since the history teachers did not have a copy of the test from which to teach, and since they had no time to complete a thorough review of the prior years' curricula, they had no idea how they were going to be able to raise their department's test scores.

The Importance of Critical Thinking in Raising Test Scores

This dilemma currently confounds teachers and administrators throughout the country. How do teachers teach what's on the test when they don't know what's on the test, and when "teaching to the standards" is insufficient? Unfortunately, if you simply rely on teaching "facts" you will always face a hit-or-miss situation in terms of covering the material that is on the test. However, if you change your strategy to teach students "how to think," they can eventually find the correct answers even if they did not study the exact material being questioned.

Critical thinking is a skill. Students can be taught how to think. Unfortunately, given today's testing mania, too many teachers rely on rote memorization and computation (lower-level thinking skills) instead of having students learn the deeper meaning of concepts (higher-level, critical thinking skills).

Here's an actual example of this dilemma:

A sixth-grade girl was asked if she could find the answer to this problem:

$$\frac{1}{2} + \frac{1}{3} + \frac{1}{6} = ?$$

The girl quickly answered, "Sure." She easily determined common denominators and gave the correct answer:

$$\frac{3}{6} + \frac{2}{6} + \frac{1}{6} = \frac{6}{6} = 1$$

Then the girl was shown the following figure and asked to explain it:

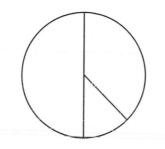

Again, she assured the teacher that she had no problem with this question. As she pointed to each section, she explained, "That's the biggest third, there's the middle third, and this is the smallest third."

It's obvious that this student knew how to compute fractions. However, she didn't understand the *concept* of fractions. Given a set of numbers, she could compute them. But given a picture that incorporates the core concepts and asked to translate it into a mathematical explanation, she experienced difficulty.

This is the dilemma that teachers face today. In an effort to cover all of the material that is to be tested, teachers too often rely on lower-level thinking skills, and too seldom focus on higher-level, critical thinking skills. The result is that if students come across a test problem that looks like something they've been taught, they'll probably get it right. However, if they come across variations of the material, or if they are given word or picture problems that require higher-level thinking skills, they are often confused and unable to find the correct answer.

The SAT exam is an excellent example of a test of students' critical thinking skills. The authors of the SAT are not as concerned about what a student knows as they are about how well the student thinks—how adept he or she is at finding the right answer, even if the student hasn't "learned" it. (For a detailed description of how to succeed at tests that focus on critical thinking, see "Teaching Study and Testing Skills," page 34).

Here's an example of a type of problem that shows up on the SAT:

Find the area of the figure on the graph:

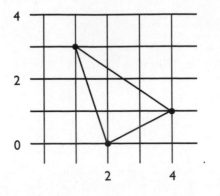

The possible answers are given:

    a. 1.15
    b. 3.48
    c. 5.76
    d. 7.25
    e. 9.98

In about five minutes, a student should be able to figure out the answer by using both the distance and Heron's formulas. Unfortunately, each SAT question is supposed to take no longer than two minutes to figure out, with an average of one minute of work time. However, if the student understands the concept of area, he or she can quickly guess the correct answer by making the following determinations:

Number of squares used in the second column of the graph: approximately 1
Number of squares used in the third column of the graph: approximately 2
Number of squares used in the fourth column of the graph: approximately ½
Total number of squares used in the figure: approximately 3½

Answer "b" is the one that is close to 3½. The point here is that if the test makers wanted to determine whether the student *knew* the correct answer, the answers provided would have been within decimal points of each other. Instead, they wanted to determine whether or not the student could use critical thinking skills to find the correct answer. In this instance, computational skills were not necessary—knowledge of the concept of area was important.

All students can provide correct answers if they learn the exact material that is covered in the test. Unfortunately, you don't always know what's on the test. Your task is to show students how to find the correct answer even when they aren't familiar with the exact problem that is presented. Good critical thinking skills allow students to do that.

Incorporating Critical Thinking into the Curriculum

A great many books have been published on the sole topic of incorporating critical thinking skills into the curriculum. The balance of this section discusses some very basic teaching methodologies that can be used to foster critical thinking skills across the curriculum.

Probably the most important way that critical thinking is incorporated into a curricululm is through the use of teacher questioning techniques. It has been proven that students respond directly to the critical thinking level that the teacher is using (Mandel 1991). The last thinking level used by a teacher when asking a question or providing direction is the thinking level that students will employ to complete the task.

Consider the following transcript of a cooperative work group lesson in which the teacher had various types of interactions with students at different stages of the work group experience. The categories of thinking levels listed below are derived from one of the easiest tools to use when referring to critical thinking categories, B. S. Bloom's *Taxonomy of Educational Objectives* (Bloom 1956).

Task Area	Thinking Level	Examples
Initial Discussion	Teacher: Knowledge	T: What do you need to know about getting food?
	Student: Knowledge	S: How they did it. And what materials they used to do it?
Directing Next Data Collection	Teacher: Comprehension	T: Are you looking for the questions or the answers first? [Leaves group]

Continued on next page

Task Area	Thinking Level	Examples
Directing Next Data Collection (continued)	Student: Comprehension	S: We have to make up our own questions and then we have to answer them ourselves—like what the farmers used for farming? Now I get it. We're not supposed to answer them yet. These are just questions we're writing down so we can get an idea.
Checking on Data Collection	Teacher: Analysis	T: Look at the topics and see if you want your topics to overlap each other, or do you want your topics to be totally separate. Look what you have so far.
	Student: Analysis	S: [Discussing pros and cons of overlapping] We'll look up different things. One of us could look up equipment. We could look up things they used for cooking, one for finding food.
Evaluating Work and Decisions	Teacher: Evaluation and Analysis	T: Try fitting all your questions into those categories. Rearrange your questions and see if it works. [Leaves group]
	Student: Evaluation and Analysis	S: What shall we put in "cooking"? Would "cooking" and "cooking equipment" be together? . . . Now we're going to put what they used for cooking into that section [group continues to analyze topics and questions]

Mandel 1991, pp. 134–136

You need to be constantly aware of the critical thinking level of your questions and directions. This is not an easy task, considering the complexity of the overall classroom environment. However, you can ensure that you incorporate the various levels of critical thinking by planning some of your discussion questions in advance.

Again, Bloom's *Taxonomy of Educational Objectives* offers what is probably the easiest and best-known way to organize critical thinking questions. Bloom divides thinking into six categories:

Higher Order	Evaluation	Appraise, judge, criticize, decide
	Synthesis	Produce, propose, design, plan, combine, formulate, compose, hypothesize, construct
	Analysis	Connect, relate, differentiate, classify, arrange, check, group, distinguish, organize, categorize, detect, compare, infer
	Application	Apply, solve, experiment, show, predict
Lower Order	Understanding	Translate, interpret, explain, describe, summarize, extrapolate
	Knowledge	Define, recognize, recall, identify, label, understand, examine, show, collect

Presseisen 1985, p. 44

Please note that one level of thinking does not necessarily follow the previous level. People do not necessarily proceed in an orderly manner from knowledge to understanding to application to analysis to synthesis to evaluation. The categories intertwine with one another throughout the thinking process.

You can prepare some basic questions in each category as part of your lesson plan. This ensures that all levels of thinking are covered at some point in the discussion. Additional questions will automatically arise as the discussion continues.

The following is an example of this process using the four major tested subject areas: language arts, math, history, and science.

Language Arts: Questions About the Short Story "The All-American Slurp" (Namioka 1987)

Evaluation	How do you think the Gleason family treated the Lin family? Give reasons for your position using examples from the story.
Synthesis	Create a short story about the Lin family's adventures during their first visit to a huge shopping mall in the United States.
Analysis	How do you think the author feels about immigrants coming to the United States?

Continued on next page

Application	Remembering what happened in the restaurant, what would have happened if the family had gone to a baseball game for the first time?
Understanding	Give an example of one problem the family had with their new life in America.
Knowledge	Where did the immigrant family come from?

Math: Questions About Common Denominators

Evaluation	Show why the multiplication of fractions results in smaller answers than does the division of fractions.
Synthesis	How would you explain your methods of analysis and application?
Analysis	How much larger is $\frac{1}{3}$ than $\frac{1}{4}$?
Application	$\frac{1}{3}, \frac{2}{7}, \frac{3}{8}$—put these in order from smaller to larger.
Understanding	Why is $\frac{1}{3}$ larger than $\frac{1}{4}$?
Knowledge	Is $\frac{1}{3}$ larger than $\frac{1}{4}$?

History: Questions About the Causes of Slavery in America

Evaluation	Take the position of a landowner in a Northern state. Write an an article defending your position on slavery. Now write an article defending your position on slavery as a landowner in a Southern state.
Synthesis	What's the relationship of economy, climate, geography, and slavery in both the North and the South?
Analysis	Which of the South's arguments for slavery were based on facts? Which were based on opinion?
Application	Predict what would have happened if the Industrial Revolution (i.e. the invention of the cotton gin) had occurred fifty years earlier than it did.

Understanding	Why did the South believe it needed slavery?
Knowledge	Which states had the most slaves?

Science: Questions About Photosynthesis

Evaluation	Defend this position using scientific reasoning: the destruction of the rain forest will severely hurt human existence.
Synthesis	How could you create an experiment to test the hypothesis that animals are healthier with plants in their environment than without (discounting plants that they use for food)?
Analysis	Inside many new large office buildings are gardens, trees, and skylights. Why do you think architects do this? (It's not just to make it pretty.)
Application	What would happen if you planted a garden in a wooded area where the trees kept everything shady all of the time?
Understanding	Why is photosynthesis important to both plants and animals?
Knowledge	What is photosynthesis?

Critical thinking can also be incorporated in the teaching of elective subjects such as art. For example, you might show students paintings by two different artists such as Chagall and Monet. (See "Teaching with the Curricular Materials You're Given" [page 13] for ways to quickly locate images of famous paintings online.) These images can either be projected from a computer onto a screen for all students to view as a class or printed for class or individual student use. The following questions can be used to raise students' critical thinking levels as they study these two paintings and create their own.

Art: Questions Related to the Comparison of Works of Art

Synthesis	Create two pictures or paintings using each of these two styles.
Evaluation	Explain the choices you made in reproducing each of the two styles. Which do you prefer, and why?

Continued on next page

Analysis	Distinguish between the styles of the cubists and the impressionists based on the two artists' paintings.
Application	Explain the different distinctive components of each of the paintings.
Understanding	Explain what you believe is happening in each painting.
Knowledge	What do you see in each painting?

Teaching Students How to Think

As was stated earlier, critical thinking can be taught. Here is an example of this process using an easy math word problem. This exercise demonstrates one procedure that you can use to instill critical thinking skills in students:

> *Juan is twice as old as Maria. In four years he will be three years older than Maria. How old is each one now?*

◎ **Pinpoint the key words or phrases.** The first step in problem solving is to pinpoint the key words or phrases that determine the answer. This is applicable to all problems in all disciplines. This procedure is also vital when reading any type of test question. Words such as all, some, none, not, except, and but are considered key words when they show up in a test question.

To solve a problem such as this one, however, more is required than a simple awareness of tricky words. The key words or phrases in this problem are:

> *Juan is **twice** as old as Maria. In four years he will be **three years older** than Maria. **How old** is **each** one **now**?*

◎ **Determine what the key words or phrases mean or imply.** Students should understand the meaning and implication of key words before they continue with the problem. Often this is the forgotten step that leads to incorrect answers. For instance, if the word *except* is included in a multiple-choice question, the student needs to know that there will be three or four correct answers given and only one incorrect answer. The *incorrect* answer is the one to mark.

In our problem, the information given implies that both the current and future ages of Juan and Maria are to be compared.

◎ **Compare what students know to what they don't know.** Every problem either provides or implies required data or other information. Students need to know how to ascertain both stated and implied information. For a simple test question, this may be a quick mental exercise. For more complicated problems, creating a chart may be helpful.

The following chart displays what students know and what they don't know in our problem:

Know	Don't Know
Juan is presently twice as old as Maria	How old each is now
He will be three years older than her in four years	

◎ **Use a "guess and check" method or some other method to relate what is known and what is not known.** The age of your students and the complexity of the problem determine how you carry out this step. Guess and check is an excellent method for beginning lessons in problem solving, regardless of students' age. More advanced students can make algebraic or logical equations to set up the relationships.

Here the guess and check method is illustrated. What students don't know is the *guess*; what they do know is the *check*. A five-column chart displays all of the information required:

Juan's Age	Maria's Age	Is Juan Twice as Old as Maria?	Their Ages in 4 Years	Is Juan Now 3 Years Older than Maria?

Next, have students make logical guesses and checks to see if a guess is correct. Start with the lowest possible answer, i.e., Maria is currently one year old and Juan is two years old. If these ages do not lead to a "yes" answer in the last column, another guess is attempted.

As soon as the information is confirmed correct (the last column), the problem is completed.

Juan's Age	Maria's Age	Is Juan Twice as Old as Maria?	Their Ages in 4 Years	Is Juan Now 3 Years Older than Maria?
2	1	Yes	J-6/M-5	No
4	2	Yes	J-8/M-6	No
6	3	Yes	J-10/M-7	Yes

Using the guess and check method, the student quickly discovers that the correct answer is that Juan is currently six years old and Maria is currently three years old.

More important, by looking at the chart the student can soon see a pattern that can be confirmed with further guesses. With older students, the teacher can demonstrate how to solve the same problem algebraically:

$$x = \text{Maria's age}$$
$$2x = \text{Juan's age}$$
$$x + 4 = \text{Maria's age in 4 years}$$
$$2x + 4 = \text{Juan's age in 4 years}$$

Your variables come from what you don't know and certain information in the problem. What is left over is the equation:

In four years Juan will be three years older than Maria. Therefore:

$$2x + 4 = (x + 4) + 3$$
$$2x + 4 = x + (4 + 3)$$
$$2x + 4 = x + 7$$
$$x + 4 = 7$$
$$x = 3 \ (\text{Maria's age})$$
$$2x = 6 \ (\text{Juan's age})$$

The guess and check method of problem solving can lead to seeing patterns and to developing critical thinking skills for more complex problems, such as those first encountered in algebra.

Many other simple techniques and methods can be incorporated into your teaching in order to help students develop critical thinking skills. For example, the following can be applied to most classroom discussions:

- Be sure that examples go from concrete to representational to abstract.
- Make connections from old to new whenever possible.
- Use graphic organizers to review material and to introduce new ideas and concepts.
- Use color to help stimulate thinking whenever possible.
- Incorporate as many of the multiple intelligences as possible into every discussion (see "Activating Your Students' Thinking," page 62).

As a result of these efforts, students will use higher levels of critical thinking more often; and most important, they will be able to discover the correct answers on the test, even if the questions concern material that has not been covered in class.

Concluding Thoughts

Even when teachers strictly adhere to the standards provided, they often discover that standardized tests include questions about material that has not been covered in class. In order for your students to succeed in these situations, it is critical that you develop their critical thinking skills so that they can *find* the correct answers even when they do not *know* the correct answers. Critical thinking can be incorporated into the classroom through careful teacher questioning techniques and through student practice. Most important, you can, through careful planning, teach your students how to think.

Teaching Study and Testing Skills

Grades 3–12

Time Line
Address this issue during the first two months of school and throughout the year before any test is given.

The Issue

How can I improve my students' study and testing skills so that they can do better on tests?

The Idea

Teaching study and testing skills is difficult because you really have little control over whether or not your students actually follow through with the techniques that you present. This is not an area in which they can be graded; they may or may not accept the validity of a direct connection between their studying techniques and their performance on assessments.

The key, therefore, is to convince them, in a logical manner, that by following your advice in this matter they will be rewarded. If your students believe that it is important to succeed on their tests, they will be more apt to listen to advice on study and test-taking skills.

The material in this section should be presented in a classroom discussion format using practical examples from both their texts and potential testing questions.

How to Study for a Test

Like athletic and artistic skills, study and test-taking skills must be both learned and practiced in order for students to master them. And mastery in these skills leads directly to higher test scores.

Ask students if they have ever spent hours studying for a test, only to get a poor grade. Why did that occur? The answer involves quantity over quality. The number of hours spent studying is not as important as the *quality* of a student's study. This is a critical point for students to understand. To put it in terms that students can appreciate, ask them if they would rather spend five hours studying and get a C, or three hours studying and get an A. Their answer should be obvious.

To start the discussion, point out that the worst way to study is to simply read over the chapter or other material to be tested a number of times. Unfortunately, this is precisely how most students study for an exam.

This concept is comparable to watching a rerun of a television sitcom episode. Although you may have paid close attention the first time you watched the episode, your attention wavers during subsequent viewings of the same episode because the plot is already familiar and you already know what each character will do and say. Reading and rereading chapters or other material to be tested is similar. The first time text is read, it is fresh to the mind. In subsequent readings, the mind already knows what words and ideas are on what page, at which spot on the page. As is the case with the sitcom rerun, it knows what's coming. The material is familiar—but not necessarily learned. However, as the student reads back over the material, the mind pays less attention because of this familiarity. In practical terms, the mind no longer pays 100 percent attention to the text. It wanders to other subjects and ideas, and studying gradually becomes inefficient. The more familiar the material becomes with each successive reading, the harder it is for the reader to concentrate on the material.

The solution is to discover various ways of manipulating the ideas and concepts in the material so that the student's brain regards the subject matter as fresh, thereby promoting better focus. Here are a few ideas on how students can study in a way that keeps the brain focused.

◎ **Make and Use Flash Cards.** Although some students may consider flash cards a waste of time, they are one of the best and most efficient ways to study key words and ideas on a test.

The student internalizes much of the information simply by physically creating the flash cards. This activity forces the student to review each bit of information to be studied as the cards are written. Each time the cards are shuffled and used, the student is exposed to the material in a new, fresh order. Flash cards can be used to study key concepts of any subject, anywhere, at any time before a test. The student can use them to quickly review information on the way to school, between classes—even while waiting for a test to begin while the teacher takes attendance. The following are some examples of flash card questions and answers from various subjects:

Science Vocabulary

PHOTOSYNTHESIS	The process used by plants to transform sunlight, water, and CO_2 into food

History Vocabulary

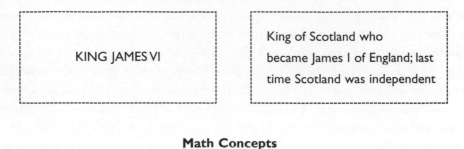

> KING JAMES VI

> King of Scotland who became James I of England; last time Scotland was independent

Math Concepts

> $(a + b)(a + b)$

> $a^2 + 2ab + b^2$

◎ **Go over textbook review questions.** Most textbooks offer review questions within chapters, at the end of each chapter, and at the end of units. Students should answer these questions, being sure to verify their answers by finding the pertinent material in the book. If the questions have been previously answered as an assignment, students should review the questions and correct any answers that were missed during the assignment. This reinforces students' learning of material that they had previously not absorbed.

◎ **Review all textbook pictures, maps, and graphs.** Students seldom study important materials such as these in preparation for tests. They should review all pictures, maps, and graphs in the text and answer the question, "Why is this here?" (The answer is not "Because it's a pretty picture"!) The authors placed these graphics in the chapter for a reason. By striving to understand these reasons, students will reinforce their knowledge of the concepts, facts, and other material presented in the text. For example, in a sixth-grade history textbook on ancient civilizations, a chapter on human adaptations contains a picture of terraced crop fields built into the side of a mountain in China. "Why is the picture here?" the student would ask. The answer is that it illustrates the text's assertion that "humans often changed the topography of the land to fit their needs." This is a major concept of this history chapter, and one that is covered in a number of questions on the chapter test.

It's critical that students understand that, to study efficiently, they need to continually review the concepts and ideas to be tested in new, fresh ways. *Efficient* study is a matter of quality, not of quantity.

Test-Taking Strategies

Like studying, test-taking is also a skill, and all skills must be practiced as much as possible in order to achieve mastery. Unfortunately for students, this means undertaking numerous tests throughout the year. This does not imply that you should now rely solely on test scores to grade students' performances. The percentage of the total grade attributed to testing should remain the same. (This may become problematic if you grade by a point system. Refer to "A Beginner's Guide to Figuring Grades" in *The New-Teacher Toolbox*, Mandel 2003.)

Students face two main types of tests: multiple-choice and short or long essays. Each question on multiple-choice tests includes a number of answers from which to choose. In essay exams, answers are entirely student generated. The following are some very basic concepts to help students excel at both multiple-choice and essay tests. (Detailed strategy guides for these types of assessments can be located in most SAT or ACT preparation books.)

◎ **Multiple-choice.** Multiple-choice questions are found on all standardized tests. Success at these assessments results from honing the skills of process of elimination and use of context clues. Students also must remember that these tests generally have set time limits. Therefore, they need to learn how to scan through the test initially to determine the questions they know, those that they can probably figure out with some effort, and those for which they have no clue and must therefore attempt to answer using both process of elimination and context clues.

For example, students should learn to follow this simple process whenever they first begin a multiple-choice test:

1. Read each question. Answer any questions to which you immediately know the correct answer.
2. Draw a small check mark next to those questions that you feel you will be able to answer given a bit of time and effort.
3. Draw a small "X" next to those questions that you believe you will have to guess at.

Using this system, students will go through the entire test and immediately answer every question they know. Then, they will go back and deal with the questions that have been marked with check marks (taking care not to spend too much time on any question). Finally, they will go through the test a third time and try to answer each question that has been marked with an "x," using both process of elimination and context clues. Obviously, the more of these last types of questions that students can answer correctly, the higher the test scores will be.

In multiple-choice exams, students must realize that success is not dependent on *knowing* the right answer, but on knowing how to *find* the right answer among the choices that are given. By learning how to use the process of elimination to make an educated guess, students will achieve higher test scores. For example, give students this problem, which has been adapted from a standardized test:

What is the currency of the former country of Yugoslavia?

    A. dollar
    B. pound
    C. lira
    D. dinar
    E. peso

Most students will select D—not because they knew the answer, but because, through process of elimination, they determined that all of the other choices were incorrect. (The correct answer is in fact D.) Students need to learn how to do this on a regular basis.

Most national standardized tests have been rigorously tested for validity and reliability before they are put into use. In selecting potential answers for each question, the authors typically include two that are definitely incorrect, one that seems possibly correct, one that seems probably correct, and one that is definitely correct. When the correct answer is not immediately known, students should determine which answers are incorrect. It is through this process of elimination that students may determine the correct answer.

Context clues can also help students figure out the answer to a difficult test question. Knowledge of prefixes and suffixes greatly assists in this process. For example, have students try to answer the following question:

The reader could not understand the article because the author was _____ in his discussion.

    A. categorizing
    B. incomprehensible
    C. reiterating
    D. editorializing
    E. summarizing

One context clue in this situation is the "negativity" of the question ("The reader could not understand"). Scanning the potential answers, students would see that only one features a negative prefix (in). None of the others contain such a prefix. Therefore, an intelligent guess would be *incomprehensible*, since the negative answer would most likely fit the negative statement. Students should locate such context clues to help determine the correct answers to questions when the process of elimination has not worked.

Obviously, the best testing scenario is one in which students know the correct answers and have no need to use process of elimination or context clues. When students actually know the material, test questions are easy to correctly answer. However, in the event that students do *not* know the answer to a multiple-choice question, they can greatly improve their odds of answering it correctly (and raising their test scores) by first using the process of elimination to get rid of answers that they know are wrong, then by using context clues to locate the correct answer.

® **Short or long essays.** Many students seem to look at essay questions in horror. They should realize, if they have studied well, essay questions are quite easy to answer. In reality, students usually get hung up on the organization of their answers rather than on the information itself. Therefore, the best way to practice essay questions is to work on students' organization skills.

First, demonstrate to your students how to simply make a list of the various answers or ideas they want to include in their essays before they start to write the essays themselves. Consider the following short essay question as an example:

> *What were the basic reasons why slavery took hold in the South, but not in the North?*

On scratch paper, or in the margins of the test, students should jot down any pertinent ideas that come to mind. For example:

North	South
North	*South*
small farms	good soil
poor soil	plantation
	labor needed
	indentured servants—no
	African slaves—yes

Once a basic list is constructed, the student can then quickly prioritize the answers so that there is a logic to the organization of his or her response. (Point out to students that organization of essays is extremely important not only in terms of making sure the information flows in a logical manner, but also in terms of making life easier for you, the teacher, who has to grade one hundred essay questions at a sitting. If you see that a student's essay is organized, you may be more favorable in your grading of that essay.)

Based on both the order of subjects as they are presented in the question (the South is mentioned before the North) and the chronological order of the events that the student wants to address, the student's list would be numbered as such:

North	South
North	*South*
7-small farms	1-good soil
6-poor soil	2-plantation
	3-labor needed
	4-indentured servants—no
	5-African slaves—yes

Once this numbering is completed, writing a short, complete essay is easy.

Make sure that students always include the question as the topic sentence of the essay:

Slavery took hold in the South but not the North mostly because of the land. The South had very good soil, which led to large plantations. Southerners needed workers for these plantations. First they used indentured servants, but these people often either finished their service terms and left or ran off, and they could not be found easily. African slaves were permanent workers, so plantation owners favored their use because they didn't have to worry about losing their work force. In the North the soil was poor. Most Northern landowners had only small farms, and they had no need for workers or slaves.

Notice how, once ideas are ordered, the points naturally flow into a full paragraph.

Caution students to read over completed essays to make sure they make sense, and to correct any errors that can be located.

After these testing strategies are incorporated, one last skill needs to be practiced. Students need to learn how to effectively check their test answers. Much to students' dismay, checking their work does not mean simply reading over the answers. Doing so often leads to nothing more than a "yeah, that makes sense" response. The best way to check answers is to physically cover the previously selected answer, mentally work through the question again, and check to see if they arrived at the same answer both times. If they do, great. If they do not, students must pinpoint the problem and provide the correct answer. Often there are clues in the latter part of a test that would result in a different answer when reviewing earlier selections. By reviewing each question, these problems can often be found.

Teacher Tool

Outlining the Chapter

Outlining is an excellent study-aid activity that few students undertake on their own. However, the teacher can regularly assign this activity for each chapter to be tested. Using chapter headings and subheadings, along with the basic material in the chapter, students can create an outline of the chapter. This accomplishes two important things. First, it requires students to actively read and work with the material. Second, outlines display the relationships among concepts, thereby helping students achieve a greater understanding of the topics presented.

Chapter outlines can also be used to create flashcards—another tool that ensures that all important material is learned.

Studying Holistically

Just as athletes must take their environment and their entire bodies into consideration when training for success, so must students approach test-taking skills in a holistic manner. By attending to both their environment and their physical well-being, they raise the probability of their success during exams.

◎ **Managing the Study Environment.** Most students say that they study on their beds, lying down, often with the stereo or television turned on (a statement that leads to teachers cringing). A couple of questions to pose might be:

> "How does a football team prepare before a huge game?"
> or
> "How does an actor rehearse the day before opening night?"

Possible answers include the wearing of full uniforms or costumes and the practicing of actual football plays or lines in a performance mode. Now ask students if a football player or an actor would prepare while wearing a T-shirt and shorts, eating pizza, or listening to the television or a CD.

Of course, the answer should be an emphatic "No!" Then why would students study in a way that does not approximate the real-life testing environment?

This concept is not an easy one for students to accept. The vast majority of them enjoy being as comfortable as possible while they do something as unpleasant as studying for a test. However, it is important that they realize the value of practicing for the testing environment. As much as they might abhor the idea, they need to sit on a hard chair at a table in a silent room while they study. Distractions must be kept at a minimum. They need to realize that, as objectionable as this may be at first, ultimately they will get used to it and be much more attuned to the actual test-taking environment. The result, of course, is higher test scores.

◎ **Preparing the body.** Again, as with athletes, there are three main aspects to having one's body in the best state possible to succeed on a test—rest, proper nutrition, and stress management. Reducing stress will be dealt with in the student part of this book.

It is imperative that your students know that they must get a good night's sleep before a test. Studying late and being groggy the following day is much less productive than studying a couple of hours less, going to bed earlier, and being fresh and alert the next day. Students need to remember that they should have already learned the majority of the material in class and during previous study sessions. Cramming a couple of extra hours of study into the evening is not going to affect their grades as much as getting a good night's sleep before an exam.

Students should also pay attention to what they eat prior to a test. Sugar (sugared cereals, candy, baked sweets, etc.) is one of the worst things they can eat within three hours of a test. Although the sugar gives them a quick high, it is followed almost as quickly by a sugar crash in which their energy goes down to levels lower than before they ate the sugar. Depending on whether the test is in the morning or the afternoon, sugar intake at breakfast or lunch needs to be monitored. Heavy meals, particularly those that include meat, should also be avoided, as they produce grogginess. Football players regularly eat complex carbohydrates before a big game. Pasta and other complex carbohydrates provide sustained, long-lasting energy.

Probably the best thing to eat is a "four square" meal—$\frac{1}{4}$ meat, $\frac{1}{4}$ vegetable, $\frac{1}{4}$ starch, and $\frac{1}{4}$ fresh fruit. This meal keeps insulin levels steady for a longer period, without highs or lows, which is most advantageous for keeping the body on-task and focused during an exam.

Meat	Vegetable
Starch	Fresh Fruit

Concluding Thoughts

Studying and test taking are critical, necessary skills that students must buy into in order to succeed on exams. As much as they may initially protest, students need to internalize the value of learning and practicing these skills if they want to do better and raise their scores. Students must learn how to study effectively and efficiently, with the emphasis on the quality, not the quantity, of study hours. They need to learn test-taking strategies in order to locate the correct answers on tests even if they don't know the particular material. Finally, they must view their study habits holistically, taking into account both their study environment and their physical state. If all of these factors are attended to, students have a greater chance of succeeding at any test.

Raising Your Morale

Grades K–12

Time Line
Address this issue two weeks before standardized tests are given, and throughout the testing period.

The Issue

How can I keep up my morale during testing so that it doesn't affect my students?

The Idea

Numerous studies have shown that teacher morale—both positive and negative—directly affects student achievement (see Black 2001 and Green 2000). In a 2004 *Education World* survey of teachers, 94.1 percent of the respondents said that teaching had become much more or moderately much more stressful during the previous five years. When you think about it, it really does make sense. If you are not happy with what you are doing in the classroom or school, it is quite difficult to excite your students in the educational process.

Low morale is even more prevalent during the testing cycle, a time enjoyed by few. Your moods and opinions on test days will invariably transfer to many of your students. This can result in lower student test scores. Even though you may think you can hide your feelings, by the testing period at the end of the year, students have come to know you very well. They can decipher your mood within minutes, and they will react accordingly. If you display negativity toward the testing procedure, you can rest assured that a number of your students will adopt that attitude.

This section focuses on what you can do to raise your morale and that of your peers. Both are important, since your fellow staff members are often your strongest support group in the school. (For ideas on steps that school administrators can take to improve teacher and student morale, see "Creating a Positive Teaching Staff" [page 83].) Without question, the biggest morale booster for teachers during the testing cycle would be to get rid of the test, change the date until later in the year when you've covered all of the material, not test students who cannot read, or any number of additional ideas that are simply not going to happen. So let's concentrate on the items that *are* practical and doable.

Working as a Mentor Teacher

Unfortunately, due to budget cuts, many states have eliminated or decreased mentor teacher programs. However, experienced teachers (those who have four or more years of experience in the classroom) can still work as unofficial mentors to inexperienced teachers. This arrangement benefits everyone on the staff. First and foremost, it helps the new teacher cope with the testing regimen, which results in higher test scores in that classroom, which improves the overall scores of the school. That makes everyone look good.

It is important for experienced teachers to look at the school from a holistic perspective, for when scores are publicized by the media, they are not in the categories of "scores from students in the classes of inexperienced teachers" and "scores from students in the classes of experienced teachers." Instead, they are all lumped together—and they ultimately reflect on the entire teaching staff.

Mentoring inexperienced teachers during the testing cycle is quite easy and does not take an exorbitant amount of time. In addition, mentor teachers will likely find that using their expertise to help an inexperienced colleague raises their own morale. A teacher's years of experience can be put to good use to directly affect the performance and morale of fellow staff members, students, and other school personnel.

Here are a number of simple activities that you can undertake as a mentor to an inexperienced teacher:

◎ **Share testing tips.** Chances are you have accumulated numerous tips from years of testing experience. These include ways to make your job easier and ways to directly assist students. Share them! Many of the ideas you will share are not taught in university education or district in-service programs. These are skills and tricks that a veteran teacher learns only from years of experience in the classroom.

◎ **Review directions and procedures that are unique to the test.** The most common mistakes made by inexperienced teachers are errors in comprehending or following the directions or procedures required for a particular test. Test-specific codes, time limits, specialized directions—although given during in-service sessions before the test—can be overwhelming and missed by the new teacher, who is already feeling the stress of the entire experience. As one who has likely given this (or a similar) test for years, you know where the pitfalls lie. Share these. Following testing directions and procedures is critical in terms of a teacher's accountability, and deficiencies in this area could directly lead to disciplinary action by the administration, depending on the severity and frequency of the mistakes.

By reviewing problematic directions and procedures with the mentee, mistakes—from major gaffes, such as administering the wrong test on a particular day (i.e. the reading section instead of the math section) to minor problems, such as forgetting to alphabetize the answer sheets before turning them in (an oft-occurring irritation for test administrators)—can often be avoided.

◎ **Put the testing into perspective.** This is an extremely important concept for the mentor teacher to share with the inexperienced teacher. Because of the enhanced importance espoused by the administration, the stress level is often high for new teachers during the testing period. You need to put the entire experience into the correct perspective. New teachers need to be assured that their jobs are not on the line with this test, and that the stress of this time is not of their doing but is a result of the accountability trickling down from the district to the administration to the teachers. They need to realize that we all put up with this for a couple of weeks every year. Most important, they must understand that how students do on the test is not necessarily a reflection on their personal teaching ability.

Another way to keep the testing period in perspective is to make sure that mentees "join the real world" occasionally during the testing period. Many new teachers stay in their rooms to work during recess and lunch. As the mentor, get the mentee out of the classroom during breaks and into the teacher's lounge or other social environment at least once during each testing day.

◎ **Check in every day.** Stop by your mentee's room every morning just to check in, say hello, and see if he or she needs any help that day. It's also a good idea to stop by sometime later in the day as well, if possible. This personal touch often does more to boost an inexperienced teacher's morale than anything else. Always remind yourself what it was like when you were a new teacher.

Partnerships

Mentoring an inexperienced teacher is one type of educational partnership. Partnerships also result from working with your peers in teams and grade levels to improve test scores. Cooperating with those with whom you have common or similar students is critical in raising teacher morale for a number of reasons.

Partnerships allow you to share ideas, problems, and frustrations with others whose experiences are similar. No one knows what you are going through as well as your colleagues. Whether you congregate to share testing strategies or simply to gripe about the test, talking with others who are in the same situation is always good for morale.

Often solutions to problems that you may encounter can be worked out in small groups. For example, if you have a few students that react negatively toward one another to the point of disrupting the testing environment, "trades" of students may be able to be worked out among you, thus solving each other's problems. (For accountability purposes, be sure to clear any movement of students between teachers with an administrator first.)

Team members can also do special things to raise each others' morale during testing. Even something as trivial as receiving a piece of chocolate from a team member first thing in the morning does wonders for one's mood during testing days. By being actively aware of each others' moods and situations in regard to testing, team members can create an extremely supportive personal community, thus raising morale during this time.

Stress Reduction

As simplistic as this may sound, sometimes a bit of stress reduction is the greatest thing to help keep morale positive during a stressful testing period. Here are a couple of ideas that can be implemented easily into the life of any school staff:

- **Order in lunch**. Schedule one day during the week—the first test day, Monday, the middle day, Wednesday, or the Friday of the testing period—to have a number of teachers get together and order in lunch. The camaraderie that will result from this event will be infectious for the entire week of testing.

- **Plan a Friday happy hour or a staff party.** Arrange for a staff happy hour or party on the Friday after the testing period is completed. The anticipation of this celebration will bring smiles to staff who face testing during the upcoming week or two.

- **Tell jokes.** Mornings are usually the worst part of any testing day. Teachers often have to get to campus early to wait in line to pick up and sign out their testing materials, and they generally have their normal morning routine disrupted. Teacher morale is probably lower at this time than at any other time during the day—and that starts the testing period off poorly for students.

  Sometimes through all of the testing, all of the procedures, all of the district and administrative directives, you simply have to laugh to raise morale. Education-related jokes work well to boost spirits, especially in the morning hours before the testing procedures have begun. The Internet is a gold mine of jokes. Start each day during the testing period by making sure that a good educational joke is posted or passed out to fellow staff members. Some educational sites, such as Teachers Helping Teachers (www.pacificnet.net/~mandel), feature a teacher-oriented "stress reduction" piece every week. These pieces will ensure that you begin each day of testing with a laugh—an activity that always leads to higher teacher morale.

The following is an example of an education-related joke found on the Internet:

You might be in education if . . .

- You believe the staff room should be equipped with a Valium salt lick.
- You want to slap the next person who says, "Must be nice to work from eight to three and have your summers free."
- You believe chocolate is a food group.
- You can tell it's a full moon without ever looking outside.
- You believe "shallow gene pool" should have its own box on the report card.
- You believe that unspeakable evil will befall you if anyone says, "Boy, the kids sure are mellow today."
- When out in public, you feel the urge to talk to strange children and correct their behavior.
- Marking all As on report cards would make your life SO much simpler.
- You believe in aerial spraying of Prozac.
- You encourage an obnoxious parent to check into charter schools or home schooling.
- You've ever had your profession slammed by someone who would never DREAM of doing your job.
- You think caffeine should be available to staff in IV form.
- Meeting a child's parents instantly answers the question, "Why is this kid like this?"

Now, after reading this, isn't your mood a little better? Did you smile throughout the piece? Imagine how this would work when you begin your testing day with a laugh.

Concluding Thoughts

Teacher morale directly affects student achievement. This is especially the case during the testing period. Therefore, it is important for you to try to improve your own and your peers' morale. This can be accomplished when veteran teachers work as mentors for inexperienced teachers by sharing testing tips, reviewing directions and procedures that are unique to a test, putting the test into perspective for them, and visiting them daily. All teachers can benefit from partnerships with fellow staff members who share the same or similar students. Finally, stress reduction—be it through food, camaraderie, or daily jokes—can help raise teacher morale.

2

Working with Students

At the faculty meeting, the principal had told Ms. Conteh and the other staff members to analyze their students and try to create strategies that would raise their standardized test scores. As she sat at her desk looking through her roll book, she wondered what she could do with this very diverse group. There was John, who never exhibited much effort unless there was a grade to be earned or some sort of reward to be provided. Rachel was the opposite of John. She always strove to do the best work in the class. Unfortunately, she rarely reached her potential because the pressure she put on herself was a constant source of stress. Juan couldn't write a complete sentence, but he could describe in minute detail the action of any basketball game he ever saw. Sandra put all of her effort into art and music, and she seemed to have little aptitude for anything academic.

How could Ms. Conteh raise the test scores of each of these individual students? Questions such as this were in the minds of all of the teachers as they left the faculty meeting.

- ◉ How could they motivate their students to do their best on tests?
- ◉ How could they activate their students' thinking processes so that students would achieve higher scores on tests?

As Ms. Conteh stared at her roll book again, she wondered how much longer she would continue to teach. Was it worth it anymore?

Issues of Relevance: Motivation, Stress, and Special Needs

Grades 3–12

Time Line
Address this issue the month before and during the testing period.

The Issue

How can I motivate my students to do their best on the standardized tests?

The Idea

The previous section focused on the numerous ways that you can manipulate the educational environment in order to raise students' test scores. Unfortunately, no amount of preparation for standardized tests will improve scores if the students themselves are not motivated and cooperative. Students are the critical variable that allow you to succeed as a result of all of your preparations.

When it comes to the relationship between students' attitudes and their test-taking success, students may be grouped into three categories:

- Those that do poorly because they are stressed out as a result of the pressure to do well that is put upon them by the school staff or by themselves
- Those that do poorly because they consider the test irrelevant or unimportant, and put little effort into it as a result
- Those that do well because they see the importance of the test and seriously attempt to do their best

Regrettably, in many schools a significant number of students fall into one of the first two categories. Even though those in the first category are good, serious students, their poor performances on tests can lower the overall scores of the school as much as the negative attitudes displayed by those in the second category. It is to these two populations that this section is especially geared.

Probably the most important factor involved in getting the most out of students throughout the standardized testing process is the personal connection that is made between you and your students over the course of the school year. Each student is an individual; each classroom community is unique. The ideas and suggestions provided throughout this section need, therefore, to be altered and adapted to each student and class. The better you know your students—and incorporate that information into your planning—the better you will be able to motivate students and help them succeed.

Three of the most prominent issues that affect student performance involve motivation, stress, and special needs.

Motivating Students

Different students need different types of motivation to do their best on the standardized tests. Some do fine with purely intrinsic motivation; some need extrinsic rewards in order to respond positively. Based on your knowledge of and personal connection with your students, you and your administration need to find a mixture of both in order to reach the majority of students.

It is critical that the ideas below are adapted to your particular teaching environment and not just implemented as presented. Motivational requirements vary widely in students of different ages. What works for third graders will often not be effective with fifth graders. What motivates a sixth or ninth grader may have no effect on an eighth or eleventh grader.

Where testing is concerned, there are not many types of extrinsic motivation techniques that can be used with students. Unfortunately, the most obvious and appropriate one—a good test score—cannot be incorporated, as the scores do not reach the school until the following academic year. As a result, the majority of extrinsic motivation activities center on student attendance during the testing period.

◎ **Perfect attendance incentives.** Both throughout the school and within the classroom, incentives can be given for perfect attendance during the testing period. Special prizes can be awarded to those students who are present every day. These incentives can range from the gift of a unique eraser for primary students to a special movie, assembly, or dance for secondary students. Again, the critical component is that the prize is motivating to that age student. Otherwise, the reward is no more than an expensive act of futility.

◎ **School raffle.** Along the same lines, a school raffle can be established to reward both good attendance and high-quality effort. An activity such as a raffle is especially useful in larger schools where money factors prohibit individual attendance prizes. Often significant prizes can be acquired through solicitation of donations from local businesses. Many community members are quite willing to assist a school once they realize that their gifts will be used to motivate and reward students in connection with raising test scores.

In a school raffle, each student is given a ticket every day they show up for the test and demonstrate an acceptable amount of effort. Granted, this last variable is rather subjective. Denying a ticket for lack of effort should be used only in the more extreme cases. For example, tickets may be withheld from those students who become disruptive, do not concentrate on the test, or simply race through the exam, marking answers at random and finishing within minutes.

Once tickets have been distributed, they are placed in a central location where students can get involved in the excitement of the activity. Depending on the size or number of prizes, a public raffle can be conducted every day at lunch, on Friday of testing week, or at the end of the overall testing period. A grand prize can also be offered at the end of the testing period.

Regardless of how you conduct the raffle, the extrinsic motivation is in place. The more students show up for and cooperate during the tests, the more chances they have to win prizes.

Although extrinsic rewards work well to motivate students, intrinsic motivation to excel at the tests should be the ultimate goal. It is critical that both teachers and school administrators implement formal programs to boost intrinsic motivation in order to raise the test scores. Most students will not motivate themselves—they tend to dislike testing as much as the teaching staff does. Therefore, they need to be actively motivated by the entire school faculty.

There are many ways to motivate students intrinsically. Many of them will actually become fun, the more you get into it! Again, all motivation must be geared to the specific age and motivating factors of your particular students in order to be effective.

◎ **Establish a fun testing atmosphere.** One of the greatest intrinsic motivation techniques is to turn the testing period into a festive pep rally type of atmosphere. The fostering of school spirit can be the guide for this activity. (This is similar to getting the school riled up for a homecoming football weekend.) School testing slogans, banners, and signs can be created by both teachers and students and displayed around the campus. This program works especially well when it is developed and implemented by the leadership or student government programs in secondary schools. Specially designed items such as testing T-shirts can be created and distributed to students to increase the spirited atmosphere. Pep rallies that feature cheerleaders and the school jazz or marching band can kick off the testing week. Whatever you do, the key is to rally students and staff together so that everybody wants to do their best for the overall welfare of the school.

There are additional ways to enhance the overall testing atmosphere. In the elementary grades, special pencils that feature the school name or some type of slogan can be purchased and distributed to students for use on the tests. In middle school, the first day of testing can be celebrated with donuts after the test. These little "gifts" can greatly contribute to the festive atmosphere you are trying to establish for the testing period.

◎ **Encourage friendly competition between classes.** Individual classes or homerooms can have competitions among themselves during the testing period. Usually attendance is the easiest variable to utilize. A prize can be given to the winning team, or perhaps the "losing" teacher may be required to do something embarrassing (but fun). Although offering a reward is a form of extrinsic motivation, the pride that students feel at having their class win a competition against a rival is a great intrinsic motivator.

◎ **Identify goals.** Teachers often receive the results of the previous year's testing broken down by category. Sometimes the information is as basic as scores of each grade level on each exam; sometimes the scores of individual skills are listed. Either way, you can select one specific area for improvement and make that your goal for the entire school year.

For example, say spelling scores were lower than you would like the previous year. You can have the class concentrate more intensely on spelling throughout the year. It can be a class goal that each student improve his or her spelling score by two points on the next exam. This could lead to a student group effort to have everyone concentrate extra hard on this particular area. (Note: This effort should not diminish the time or energy spent on learning other subjects to be tested. It is simply meant as a way to motivate students to make a full-class effort to improve spelling performance.)

◎ **Buying into the importance of the test.** Students who do poorly because they consider the test irrelevant or unimportant, and therefore put little effort into their performance, are often found in the last year of elementary school or throughout middle or high school. These students feel that they will not be held accountable for, or experience negative repercussions as the result of, poor test performance.

It is important that a week or two before the test, you have a serious, realistic discussion with students about the repercussions of doing well or poorly on the end-of-year standardized tests. Students need to understand that the test is not just something that is thrown at them by the administration or school district that really doesn't affect them at all. Rather, there could be long-lasting consequences for those that do either extremely well or extremely poorly.

For those who do extremely well, there are often special rewards that are directly tied to the yearly exams. Admission into gifted programs is often determined by very high scores on the standardized test. Enrollment into honors or advanced placement courses may be based on how well a student does on these assessments. For those in the last year of elementary or middle school, the type of classes into which they are placed in the next level of school—top-level courses or remedial classes—is frequently tied to their test scores.

For those who do extremely poorly on the yearly exams, there are often serious consequences. In addition to running the risk of being placed in lower-level classes, an increasing number of schools are instituting remedial reading and math classes. These courses, which are often double-blocked over two consecutive periods, are mandatory for students who score in or near the bottom percentiles of the test. Although these students may not care about being placed in remedial classes, they should realize that by being placed in a double-block, they end up losing their elective in most cases. Courses in music, art, computers, driver's education, and other fun subjects are not available to those who have to give up an extra period for a double-blocked remedial course. This realization in and of itself is often enough to get these students to increase their efforts on the standardized tests.

Student Stress Reduction

Very often school staff—both administrators and teachers—place so much emphasis on the standardized tests that students become stressed out and subsequently underperform on the test. This is a serious problem, and it is more prevalent than most believe.

This is a different situation than using stress reduction to raise teacher morale. You should not start the test sessions with a joke, for example, because that will take students completely out of the serious mind-set that you want to instill. There are, however, a number of things that you can do to assist students who are prone to stress during end-of-the-year exams. Remember, even though the majority of students may not be affected by stress, if enough are affected, the entire school's overall scores can be significantly reduced. In addition, even those students who do not suffer from stress will benefit from these strategies.

◎ **Put the test into its proper perspective.** Stressed students need to understand that the standardized tests are not considered in their grades, and that they will most likely (depending on the population) not affect their future class placements (unless they do extraordinarily poorly as a result of making no attempt). It's also important for them to realize that test taking is a *skill*, and that they will be tested, in one way or another, throughout their lives. Throughout their educational career, students will face many tests: yearly school exams, the SAT or the ACT, a written test to obtain a driver's license, and more. You need to get students to understand that tests are one of those regular, annoying things that must be done in their lives—ranking right up there with annual trips to the dentist and cleaning their rooms. The more that students accept testing as a part of their lives, the less stress will result from the exams themselves. Discussing the issue in these terms often assists students to put the test into its proper perspective, which ultimately decreases students' stress levels.

◎ **Encourage test preparation.** Test taking is a skill. And, as with all skills, the more it is practiced, the better one becomes at taking tests. A number of professionally written test-preparation books are available for all subjects and grade levels from elementary through high school. These are excellent tools to give to students on a regular basis the month or two before the testing cycle begins. The more students practice using similar types of exams, the easier the actual test becomes.

In addition to these practice exams, teachers should give a number of different types of tests to students throughout the year. Even if you dislike the multiple-choice tests provided with your textbook, these are similar to the types of tests students will experience. This is not to say that you should give up the personally created tests that you currently use—rather, that you should also incorporate these published exams on occasion. You do students a great disservice if the first time they encounter these types of exams is during the mandatory standardized testing.

Teachers should also occasionally provide elementary and middle school students opportunities to use a Scantron-type answer sheet throughout the year. You would be surprised how many students have difficulty going from a test booklet to bubbling in the correct answer on a separate answer sheet. In elementary school especially, it is also important to remind students that being the first one to finish a test is not a sign of doing well on the test, and that it is not important.

Again, test taking is a skill, and the more practice that you can provide your students with similar test-taking situations, the more comfortable they will become with the real exam. Ultimately, these activities will pay off in the form of higher test scores.

◎ **Teach relaxation techniques.** Physical ailments such as ulcers are a growing malady that affect many high-achieving students today. Academic stress is the primary cause (Hardy 2003). By teaching students some simple stress reduction techniques, you often can assist students in lowering their stress levels. Here are a couple of simple stress-reduction activities that students can use before a test or during a break between testing sessions:

- To reduce physical stress, tighten toe muscles as much as possible and hold the pose for ten seconds. Relax the muscles, then tighten foot muscles for ten seconds. Relax those, then tighten calf muscles for ten seconds. Working upward, continue tightening and relaxing various parts of the body, including thighs, buttocks, stomach, back, hands, forearms, upper arms, shoulders, neck, face, and head. Finish by tightening all of the muscles in the body for ten seconds. After completing this exercise, students will immediately feel that their entire bodies are more relaxed.

- To reduce mental stress, close the eyes and create a mental picture of the numeral 1. Its size, shape, and color are irrelevant; the goal is to simply focus on the number. Using the word "one" as a mantra of sorts, silently and slowly repeat the word over and over. Five to ten minutes of this activity provides a great sense of relaxation. Students should be cautioned to perform this technique only when they are in a quiet, safe place, and that they might want to set an alarm to go off in ten minutes—this exercise has been known to put people to sleep as they become completely relaxed!

Testing Students with Special Needs

This section is aimed at those teachers who are required by the state or district to test students who have mild to moderate disabilities.

Many states now require teachers to test special-needs students not at the grade level at which they are working, but at the grade level in which they are officially placed. Obviously, this ensures lower test scores for the school, since the reason these students are in a special education program is because they cannot function at this level. Worse, however, is the strain that this testing puts on the self-esteem of these students when they take an exam that makes them painfully aware of their educational deficiencies. Many of these students already possess low self-esteem, and these tests only serve to compound the problem.

Unfortunately, there is little that you can do to keep special-needs students out of this situation other than try to have them exempted from the test—a practice that is increasingly becoming illegal, forbidden, or extremely difficult to accomplish. However, there are a number of ways that you can not only keep the self-esteem of these students at a higher level, but also actually raise their test scores.

◎ **Adhere to the Individualized Education Plan (IEP).** The educational goals, objectives, and accommodations of the IEP supercede all testing procedures determined by the state and the district. The IEP is a *federally* mandated legal document, and it takes precedence over all state-determined testing directives.

For example, if the IEP states that during math, the student should have the problems read out, that accommodation applies to the math section on the test. If the IEP directs you to provide extended time or breaks during an exam, then the time limitations for the standardized tests are no longer valid for that student.

◎ **Prepare your special education students for the skills required by the test.** You should work to prepare special-needs students for the testing atmosphere throughout the year.

Special-needs students often find test taking quite stressful, and they may spend an inordinate amount of time struggling with questions they cannot answer. These students need to learn to spend only a minimal amount of time on such questions and move on to the next question. Because students are not allowed to ask for assistance during the test, it is not a good idea to wait until the last minute to try to teach this skill, as this will cause tremendous frustration in the student, who may totally shut down as a result.

Review test-taking strategies with your special-needs students throughout the year, especially the multiple-choice types of questions they will encounter on the exam. One special education teacher taught her kids to determine one of the following responses for each question:

- "I really know this answer."
- "I think I can figure this out."
- "I am clueless!"

For the last response, she teaches students that rather than skip this question or spend too much time on it, they should pick a letter from the answer sheet and stick with it throughout the test, marking it whenever they encounter a "clueless" answer.

Sometimes students who have more severe disabilities need to learn and practice the very basics, such as how to fill in the bubbles on the answer sheet. Again, students should practice this weeks or months before the test in order to both improve their scores and, more important, lower their frustration levels.

◎ **Mentally prepare your special-needs students.** Have a discussion with special-needs students the week before the test in order to prepare them for what lies ahead. The goal is to get students to relax as much as possible before the testing period. Discuss with them where they started off at the beginning of the year and how far they have come since then. They need to understand that they should do whatever they can on the test. Most important, be up front with them. Your special-needs students need to realize that the test may not be fair, and that their results are not necessarily indicative of either their intelligence or their achievements.

Finally, although this is highly subjective, if you feel your special education students have done their best, treat them to something special at the end of the week, such as a fun movie. This will give them an activity to work toward, while simultaneously letting them know that you are proud of them.

As a result of all of these efforts, special-needs students will not only score a little better on the standardized tests, but also—and more important—their self-esteem will not be harmed by taking a test at which they cannot succeed because of their learning disabilities.

Teacher Tool

Testing English Learners

An increasing number of states require that English Language Learners (ELLs) take the standardized tests in English—even though they cannot read or understand the directions or questions. Many of the ideas presented in "Testing Students with Special Needs" (page 58) can be adapted to help these students. Most important, students need to understand that any failures on the test are due to their lack of knowledge regarding the English language, and *not* to any intellectual problem. This is critical in terms of keeping students' self-esteem high. Students should never be made to feel dumb because they cannot succeed at a test that they can neither read nor understand.

If ELL students are allowed to use a version of a standardized test in their native language, then all of the other test-taking strategies included in this book are applicable to them, just as they are to English-speaking students. Remember, the issue with ELL students is *language*, not basic intelligence.

Concluding Thoughts

Regardless of all your plans for raising test scores, no improvement will happen unless the students themselves cooperate. Teachers need to motivate students to do their best on the tests. This can be accomplished through activities that encourage both extrinsic and intrinsic motivation, such as attendance-incentive programs and events that foster school spirit and establish a positive testing atmosphere. Teachers also need to deal with student stress, which can reduce test scores. Putting the test into perspective, preparing students for the test, and teaching relaxation techniques all help to alleviate this problem. Finally, those who are required to test students with special needs have unique problems, because not only do these students traditionally test low, but also because their self-esteem is affected by being forced to take a test that is well beyond their abilities. Special education teachers need to make sure that the IEP takes precedence over state- or district-mandated testing procedures; that their students have learned the skills that are required to take the test, and that the students are mentally prepared for the testing experience.

Activating Your Students' Thinking

Grades K–12

Time Line
Address this issue through-out the year.

The Issue

How can I activate my students' thinking processes so that they can achieve higher scores on tests?

The Idea

Since the 1990s, a large amount of education research has focused on how students think. Researchers are attempting to discover what it is that activates their brains, and they have developed several theories in regard to that. The ultimate goal is to discover how teachers can help develop students' thought processes, thereby leading to greater student achievement.

One of the best, most popular, and easiest-to-apply of these theories is called the multiple intelligences theory (Gardner 1993, 1999). This theory holds that there are eight different ways in which students think:

- **Verbal-Linguistic.** The capacity to use words effectively in both oral and written form.

- **Logical-Mathematical.** The capacity to use numbers effectively and to reason well.

- **Visual-Spatial.** The ability to perceive the visual-spatial world accurately and to perform transformations of those perceptions; the ability to represent visual or spatial ideas graphically.

- **Bodily-Kinesthetic.** The ability to use one's body to express ideas and feelings and to use one's hands to produce or transform things. (This intelligence pertains to not only athleticism, but also to areas such as dance and drama).

- **Musical-Rhythmic.** The ability to perceive, discriminate among, express, and transform musical forms.

- **Interpersonal.** The ability to perceive distinct moods, intentions, motivations, and feelings of other people.

◎ **Intrapersonal.** Self-knowledge and the ability to act adaptively on the basis of that knowledge.

◎ **Naturalist.** The ability to recognize, discriminate among, and classify plants, animals, minerals, and other items in an individual's environment, including nonliving forms found in an urban environment (Armstrong 2000).

Activities within each category activate the mind of the person who has strong tendencies in that area. For example:

◎ A person who best internalizes new ideas through reading most likely has a high **verbal-linguistic intelligence**.

◎ A person who is adept at discovering the logic or flow of things probably has a high **logical-mathematical intelligence**.

◎ A person who best learns through pictorial or three-dimensional representations of concepts has a high **visual-spatial intelligence**.

◎ A person who does his or her best thinking while performing a physical activity, such as jogging, likely has a high **bodily-kinesthetic intelligence**.

◎ A person who performs best on tasks while listening to music most likely has a high **musical-rhythmic intelligence**.

◎ A person who best learns and performs by "talking out" new ideas with others probably has a high **interpersonal intelligence**.

◎ A person who requires time to reflect on new ideas and information in order to process this material probably has a high **intrapersonal intelligence**.

◎ A person who does his or her best thinking while outdoors has a high **naturalist intelligence**.

The multiple intelligences are areas that activate one's thinking. The key for educators is to learn how to use this theory to help activate students' thinking processes.

Using the Multiple Intelligences for Student Diagnosis

Multiple intelligences can be used to assist students in curricular areas in which they are having difficulty. For example, a fourth-grade boy was having difficulty learning his multiplication tables. Flashcards, worksheets, drilling—none of these helped. Finally, the student's teacher gave him a cassette tape that featured the times tables set to music. Within a day or two the student knew them all by heart. It was only later formally determined, however, that the boy had a very high musical-rhythmic intelligence. The music of the songs on the tape activated his thinking processes, which allowed him to learn the material much more easily. As wonderful as his teacher was, if she had known about the multiple intelligences she could have diagnosed his learning style and as a result used music to help the student learn his multiplication tables at a much earlier date.

This example illustrates the benefit of using the multiple intelligences as a student diagnostic tool throughout the year. If students are having difficulty in a curricular area or with some specific material, you can capitalize on each student's intelligence strength to assist that student in learning the material.

During the first few weeks of the school year, you should give each of your students a multiple intelligence assessment. (See the Teacher Tool sidebar below for some excellent resources on student assessments and other methods of determining a student's highest and lowest type of multiple intelligence.) Note each stu-

Teacher Tool

Here are three excellent resources for teachers who want to learn more about multiple intelligences:

• *Multiple Intelligences in the Classroom* (Armstrong 2000) is probably the best resource book on adapting the theory to every aspect of the teaching and classroom environment. It also contains a number of multiple intelligence assessments that are designed for use with students.

• Teachers' Curriculum Institute's *History Alive!* contains a couple of fantastic multiple intelligence assessments for use with elementary and middle school students.

• *Cooperative Work Groups: Preparing Students for the Real World* (Mandel 2003) offers a detailed discussion on integrating the multiple intelligences in all aspects of the classroom curricula and environment.

dent's highest form of multiple intelligence next to his or her name in the class roll book for quick and easy access.

Here are a couple of examples of how to use the multiple intelligences to best assist students. These particular examples deal with a student who is having difficulty understanding the theme of a piece of literature and a student who does not seem to understand the mathematical concept of common denominators. Often it is difficult to personalize help sessions during class time. Therefore, for this discussion, we will assume these students have come to see you for extra help after school or during a free period during the day.

Your first step is to refer to your roll book to see the student's highest intelligence area. You can then either present the material in a way that incorporates that intelligence area or manipulate the student's environment in such a way that the intelligence area is incorporated. This is a very important distinction. Not every piece of curricular material can be taught *easily* using every multiple intelligence. Let's face it—there are very few good songs for teaching quadratic equations! Therefore, you must often discover a way to activate the student's highest intelligence area by manipulating the environment in which the student learns. The following chart provides some examples for the two students mentioned above:

Intelligence	English student having difficulty with themes	Math student having difficulty with common denominators
Verbal-Linguistic	Verbally explain how the theme is derived from aspects of the text; point out sections of the written material as examples.	Verbally explain how common denominators function. Describe various examples.
Logical-Mathematical	Use a graphic organizer to show how the theme is derived; create a flowchart that demonstrates how plot events and character traits both affect and are affected by the theme.	Demonstrate how common denominators are derived using various mathematical equations.
Visual-Spatial	Use drawings, photographs, and other visual representations of the story's concepts to describe how the theme is derived.	Draw pictures of various shapes divided into fractional units. Using different colors, subdivide the shapes to represent the concept of common denominators.

Continued on next page

Intelligence	English student having difficulty with themes	Math student having difficulty with common denominators
Bodily-Kinesthetic	Manipulate the environment by creating some physical movement in the student, such as by making an excuse to walk together to the office. During the walk, discuss the concepts that are giving the student problems.	
Musical-Rhythmic	Manipulate the environment by playing some background music (use a genre that the student enjoys). Discuss the concepts that are giving the student problems.	
Interpersonal	Manipulate the environment by pairing the student up with a friend who understands the concepts that are giving difficulty. Have the two discuss the concepts.	
Intrapersonal	Have the student go home and write a diary entry for one of the characters, using the theme as the subject of the entry.	Have the student go home and analyze the day's activities by determining how many hours, then minutes, then seconds were spent on various activities.
Naturalist	Manipulate the environment by going outside and sitting on the grass or under a tree and discussing the concepts that are giving problems or finding a way to put the material into classifications in order to demonstrate relationships.	

Each student should be aware of his or her personal multiple intelligence strengths and weaknesses. This will assist them with self-diagnosis when they are having difficulty understanding curricular material. Early in the year, when the concept of multiple intelligences is first introduced, you should demonstrate how students can use their strengths to enable them to study more efficiently, especially when they encounter areas in which they are having problems.

The following chart provides various examples of what students can learn to do on their own if they experience difficulties with curricular material, depending on their personal intelligence strengths:

If the student's strongest intelligence is	The student can learn difficult or problematic material by
Verbal-Linguistic	reading material that explains the concept; talking to a classmate or adult and having that person explain it.
Logical-Mathematical	making an outline of the information; using or creating a graphic organizer; connecting aspects of the material in a flow chart or web.
Visual-Spatial	looking at pictures or other graphics that illustrate the concept; "drawing out" parts of the problem to create a pictorial representation.
Bodily-Kinesthetic	reading over the material, then immediately going out and doing some physical activity while the information is fresh in the mind; have a squeeze/exercise apparatus in hand while studying.
Musical-Rhythmic	playing non-distracting music in the background.
Interpersonal	working or studying with a friend.
Intrapersonal	stopping every so often to reflect on what is being studied; imagining oneself in a personal situation that involves the concepts being studied.
Naturalist	going outside and studying while sitting on the grass or in a natural setting.

Adapting the Testing Environment to Promote Thinking

Unfortunately, almost all testing, especially standardized testing, is entirely verbal-linguistic–based, and to a point, logical-mathematical based. Students who do poorly on such tests often are low in these two intelligences. The result: even though students may know that material, they are at an immediate disadvantage, and they will often not perform as well as they should.

Although you obviously cannot change the construction of the standardized tests, you *can* manipulate the environment to help non–verbal-linguistic and non–logical-mathematical students activate their thinking and subsequently improve their test scores. Be aware that some of the suggestions below are nontraditional. However, the goal is to improve students' test scores, and students who are high in the "nontraditional" areas of intelligence may need this extra assistance to perform up to their capabilities.

Visual-Spatial. For visual-spatial students, post pictures or posters that illustrate various aspects of the subject being tested that day. (Obviously, you need to ensure that the graphics do not provide answers to any questions on the test.) Give students scratch paper to doodle on throughout the test. Collect the paper at the end of the testing period in order to satisfy security concerns.

Bodily-Kinesthetic. Provide time for students who have a high bodily-kinesthetic intelligence to get up and walk around between test sections. Let these students keep a squeeze ball or other small handheld exercise device at their desks to use throughout testing.

Musical-Rhythmic. Have popular music playing in the classroom as students enter it. Continue to play the music until it's time to begin the test. Play music during breaks between test sections. (Note: take care not to play music so loudly that it disturbs other classes that are still testing.)

Interpersonal. Allow students who have a high interpersonal intelligence to sit next to friends, or at least near other people. Do *not* move their seats so that they are away from everybody, as is traditional in testing situations. Sitting next to someone does not mean that they will talk with that person or cheat on the test. However, physical proximity to others is often enough to stimulate the thinking processes of these students.

Intrapersonal. Allow students who are high in intrapersonal intelligence to move their seats to a corner of the room or someplace away from all distractions and all other people. If the seats are not moveable, allow the students to sit in the front corner seats, where they will have a minimum of contact with others.

Naturalist. Have students who are high in naturalist intelligence face a window (if there is nature outside to see). If this is not feasible, put them near a classroom plant or animal. If this is also not possible, have them sit near or facing a poster or picture that illustrates some aspect of nature.

Concluding Thoughts

One of the best ways to help students improve both their ability to learn and their test scores is to work on activating their unique thinking processes. Multiple intelligences theory can greatly assist you in accomplishing this goal. Through the use of multiple intelligences, you can diagnose student problems using their preferred intelligence in order to help them learn problematic material. You can also manipulate your classroom to provide a better thinking and testing environment for non–verbal-linguistic and non–logical-mathematical students, especially during standardized testing periods.

3

Administrative Concerns

This section is addressed to school administrators. Please note that *administrator*, here, refers to principals and assistant principals only. Administrators found in local or central district offices are not included in these discussions.

Mr. Phillips had just finished another faculty meeting. The principal was both mentally and physically exhausted. He had been directed by his superiors to review–*again*–the school's standardized test score data with his staff–a prospect that had been met with tremendous resistance from his teachers. Their comments had been predictable. They were tired of going over the data again and again; they were doing their best already; the year's test scores were higher than those of previous years; why weren't their efforts being appreciated? The teacher complaints continued for almost half an hour. Mr. Phillips was utterly frustrated. His faculty had little conception of what he was going through personally. He had to raise the school's scores enough to satisfy his downtown bosses. If he couldn't, he faced sanctions or a transfer. He had to demonstrate to the parents and community that their school was improving, and, at the same time, he had to make his teachers happy. All of this had to be accomplished while dealing with a student population that was traditionally low-performing.

Mr. Phillips and his fellow principals across the district pondered their dilemma that afternoon. They knew their schools' scores were steadily improving, but the improvements didn't seem to satisfy anyone. All of these administrators were struggling with the same situation.

- How could they show the real improvement of the school's test scores?
- How could they keep up the morale of their teachers during testing so that poor morale didn't affect students?
- How could they set up a system of administering both the tests and the testing environment in order to get the most out of students?

As Mr. Phillips reviewed the data again, he wondered how much longer he would continue as a principal. Was it worth it anymore?

Dealing with Test Scores: On Site and with Parents

Grades K–12

Time Line
Address this issue throughout the school year (especially at the beginning of the year) whenever test scores are discussed by the faculty or publicized by the media.

The Issue

How can I show the real improvement of the school's test scores?

The Idea

Probably more than teachers, you principals face tremendous pressure to raise your schools' test scores. Superintendents, ever mindful of public perception of the quality of local schools, place immense pressure on their principals to improve. Too often you are threatened with transfer or demotion if score goals are not met on an annual basis. Unfortunately, unlike teachers, principals rarely have strong unions that will help you keep your jobs. Too often you must focus on the improvement of test scores in your school as if your job depended on it—and, too frequently, that is indeed the case.

Administrators, albeit ultimately responsible for the overall academic success of the entire student body, need to deal with the effects of the end of-the-year standardized testing in various ways. First and foremost, where schoolwide test scores are concerned, you need to deal with the staff on site and the general parent community.

Interpreting the Scores

Probably the single most important concern regarding the issue of raising test scores is how the scores are actually reported and, more important, interpreted. Frequently schools that improve their scores find that the reports indicate no improvement. This is because scores are usually reported and discussed in terms of percentiles.

⊚ **The problems with percentiles.** The use of percentiles to measure school progress is a significant problem for many institutions. Percentiles are inherently unfair to those schools in low socioeconomic areas where student achievement is problematic due to either large non-English speaking immigrant populations or poor economic conditions.

Percentiles rank school scores in comparison to those of all the other schools that administer the same statewide exam. The schools that score in the lower 10 percent on the state exam will fall into the first percentile. The schools that rank in the 11- to 20-percent range fall into the second percentile, and so on, up to the tenth percentile. Unfortunately, school demographics or location are not taken into account.

The problem with this ranking system is that even when a school improves its scores, that improvement may not be evident if every other school's scores also improve. With percentiles, no matter how much each school succeeds in raising its scores and improving student achievement, one school will always be ranked at the bottom.

Consider the following scenario: a number of schools in an urban, lower socioeconomic area score extremely low on the state exam. The entire district institutes a new reading program, one that has students reading two hours every day. Lo and behold, the reading test scores of every school in the district improve the next year. However, although the low-performing schools' scores significantly increase, those schools are *still* ranked near the bottom of the district—because every other school improved as well. Even though the teaching and administrative staff did a great job at improving their students' scores, that improvement is not recognized—in fact, it may be belittled—because their schools still rank near the bottom of all schools in the district.

For schools that have a significant immigrant population of students who are not fluent in the English language, this is an exceedingly unfair result. For schools that are in an economically deprived area where students have not had the resources or background to allow them to excel, this is an exceedingly unfair result.

Morale very often becomes lower at such schools, which contributes to a culture of failure. Staff and students gradually come to believe that, regardless of their best efforts and because of factors well beyond their control, their school is still considered—and will always be considered—a low performer.

It is important to stress that it is also beyond the control of administrators to change the way in which scores are presented by the state, the district, or local media. However, they can work to ensure that their individual school's achievement is publicized and promoted to reflect the real improvement and accomplishment that exists.

◎ **Use raw scores to show actual improvement.** A school's actual improvement is displayed in its precise numeric raw score. A school whose score has gone from a 320 to a 385 has improved not only sixty-five points, but has demonstrated a 20 percent increase in its scores! That is a huge improvement, even if the school is still considered to be in the lowest percentile overall for its district.

As long as the raw scores are based on the same scale from year to year (i.e., the entire test may be worth eight hundred points every year), you can legitimately use the data to compare one year's achievements to the next.

Here is an example illustrating how these two systems of reporting progress differ, using a couple of inner-city, lower-socioeconomic-area schools. The following chart provides a comparison of the same results using both raw scores and percentiles over a two-year period:

Previous Year's Raw Score	Previous Year's Percentile Within District	This Year's Raw Score	This Year's Percentile Within District	Real Improvement in Raw Score
285	1	330	1	45 points— 16 percent
289	1	295	1	6 points— 2 percent

The first school showed significant improvement in its test scores from one year to the next, whereas the second school demonstrated little improvement. However, because the district average for this test is 475 points, both schools remain in the bottom percentile, and it therefore appears as if neither school improved to any real degree.

Obviously, this is blatantly unfair to the first school. Even worse, the subsequent negative perceptions of that school can ultimately become a morale issue for its faculty members, who worked tirelessly—and successfully—to improve their students' test scores, only to find their efforts virtually unappreciated. Why should teachers continue to strive to improve test scores when even significant achievements are discounted or ignored? The difference in raw scores from year to year is the true indication of student improvement. It is therefore up to the administration to actively promote this positive information when discussing the school's performance with staff, the district, and the parents of the community— even if the media, the state, and the district itself refuse to do so.

◎ **Put the scores into perspective.** A major flaw in the discussion of a school's test scores comes when totally dissimilar schools are compared to each other. It results in an exercise that is analogous to comparing apples to oranges. Demographics have a tremendous amount of influence over both the actual and the realistic potential of students' performances on the standardized tests. This variable needs to be put into perspective whenever discussing test scores. This is especially the case when a comparison is being made between schools.

Refer to the following example. In this state, each school is scored on a test-based scale, with a perfect score being eight hundred. This is the scale by which all schools in the state, including those within this urban district, are judged. The following chart was presented to the staff at Kennedy Middle School at the beginning of the year. The chart shows how that school compared to the other middle schools in their particular region of the city.

School Name	Last Year's Score	School Name	This Year's Score
Johnson Middle School	789	Johnson Middle School	790
Taft Middle School	625	Taft Middle School	630
Kennedy Middle School	480	Lincoln Middle School	504
Lincoln Middle School	476	McKinley Middle School	500
Hoover Middle School	450	Kennedy Middle School	496
McKinley Middle School	440	Hoover Middle School	445
Wilson Middle School	323	Wilson Middle School	333
Jefferson Middle School	275	Jefferson Middle School	330
Adams Middle School	220	Adams Middle School	300

The staff at Kennedy Middle School was admonished for their poor performance in relation to the other schools in the region. The following issues were stressed in the subsequent discussion:

- Their school fell from third to fifth in the region
- Their school improved by only sixteen points, compared to the sixty-point increase shown by McKinley and the eighty-point increase achieved by Adams

This was a very disturbing session for the teachers at Kennedy, because they had met their district-established personal goal of improving by at least fifteen points. In fact, the school had actually improved its scores each year for the past eight years. Finally, someone pointed out the significant demographic differences between the schools that were presented in the table:

School Name	Demographics of the School
Johnson Middle School	Upper–middle-class socioeconomic area
Taft Middle School	Upper–middle-class socioeconomic area
Kennedy Middle School	Significant immigrant and minority population; lower-class socioeconomic area
Lincoln Middle School	Mixture of low- and middle-income families
Hoover Middle School	Mixture of low- and middle-income families
McKinley Middle School	Upper–middle-class socioeconomic area
Wilson Middle School	Mixture of low- and middle-income families
Jefferson Middle School	Significant immigrant and minority population; low socioeconomic area
Adams Middle School	Significant immigrant and minority population; low socioeconomic area

By taking these demographic factors into account with the original chart above, the following items were now singled out for consideration:

- The only schools with similar students to those at Kennedy were Jefferson and Adams, both of which achieved significantly less improvement than Kennedy.

- The scores at Adams went up as much as they did because they were so low to begin with; this was the first time the school had shown significant improvement in five years.
- Compared to other schools with the same socioeconomic environment, McKinley had been a serious underperformer, and had just this year achieved the score it should have achieved all along.
- How has Kennedy been doing such a great job in performing so much higher than these other schools in better socioeconomic areas?

This is the type of analysis and discussion that administrators need to present. The fact is, given the demographics and the socioeconomics of its students, the staff at Kennedy are doing an excellent job at raising test scores. Can they improve the school's scores even more? Obviously. Should they settle for the scores they currently achieve? Of course not. But will they ever achieve the type of scores that Johnson and Taft enjoy? It's highly unlikely. For the sake of both staff and student morale, as well to garner positive publicity for the school, it is important to point out how well this school's students, staff, and administration have been doing in raising their test scores.

Many elementary schools analyze scores by comparing past and current year's scores by grade level. This, too, is problematic. It is important to compare scores by specific groups of students, not by grade levels. Groups of students often vary greatly from one year to another. Ask any classroom teacher; it's easy to tell differences between students from different years.

Consider the following as an example of this phenomenon:

	Year One	Year Two	Year Three
Fifth Grade	354	358	342
Fourth Grade	355	335	342
Third Grade	331	344	344

By looking at scores by grade level, the following would appear evident:

- Fifth-grade students did much worse in year three compared to year two.
- Fourth-grade students did much worse in year two than in year one, but they rebounded in year three

However, when the results are viewed in terms of specific groups of students advancing from one grade level to the next over the three years, the interpretations are significantly different. The arrows in the chart below display the movement of the same group of students:

	Year One	Year Two	Year Three
Fifth Grade	354	358	342
Fourth Grade	355	335	342
Third Grade	331	344	344

The third-grade students in year one become the fourth-grade students in year two and the fifth-grade students in year three. The third-grade students in year two become the fourth-grade students in year three. When you look at the scores in this fashion, the results seem quite different:

- The scores of the fifth graders in year three have steadily improved every year. More important, they have been a traditionally low-performing class. Therefore, there was no "real" drop in fifth-grade test scores.
- The fourth graders in year three did not actually do better than they had during the previous year, when they were third graders. Instead, those students' scores fell.

Sometimes specific grade levels have unique situations that must be taken into account. For example, a number of years ago a large, urban school district eliminated social promotion in the second and fifth grades. The result was that in one year, many low-performing students were retained, resulting in fewer low-scoring students entering the next grade level and more low-scoring students staying at the same grade level. This skewed two grade levels' test-score results not only the following year, but also each subsequent year of these students' progression, all the way through high school. Factors such as this must be taken into account when analyzing test scores.

It's important for both the morale of the school staff and the reputation of the school that administrators and teachers do not compare apples and oranges. Instead, it is imperative that the analysis and discussion of test scores be placed into their correct perspective.

Positive Public Relations

Promoting the success of the school concerning test scores is an important action that is not always explored by administrators. This is because too often, a school's scores—at least as they are presented by the state or the district—are not something its principal wants to publicize. However, once you analyze the scores in a way that makes sense, you may find good reason to be proud of your school's academic programs. Following are ways in which you can promote the real achievements of your school:

◎ **Present the test scores to the community.** Consider again the situation faced by the administrators of Kennedy Middle School (see page 74). At first glance, this year's scores were disheartening. The school was ranked in the second percentile, significantly below top schools in the region. In fact, the school's scores seemed to have worsened compared to others in its region.

However, by putting the scores into proper perspective, the staff realized that it had some excellent bragging points:

z Kennedy Middle School scores increased for the eighth straight year. This year's scores were, in fact, 7 percent higher than their established district goal.

z Kennedy Middle School scores are 53 percent higher than the next highest score from a school in its neighborhood.

Both of these statements place the school's scores in their correct perspective and provide a foundation for positive public relations.

◎ **Get the word out about your school.** It is disappointing that many journalists in the local media accentuate the negative when it comes to the achievements of public schools. It is therefore incumbent on the administration to publicize the positive information that is gleaned from their test-score analysis whenever possible. Achievements create respect for a school. And respect often translates into increased material support from businesses and more favorable public attitudes toward bond issues. There are a number of ways to accomplish this exercise in public relations.

Send a press release to local newspapers immediately after the scores are released. This can be developed by school staff or by a parent who is active in the school. Here's an example of an appropriate short but effective press release:

PRESS RELEASE

Kennedy Middle School Continues Its Steady Improvement

Kennedy Middle School raised its standardized test scores for the eighth straight year. Not only did it exceed its district-established goal by 7 percent, but it also continues to surpass all other middle schools in the area. In fact, Kennedy scores were a remarkable 53 percent higher than those of its closest neighbor.

For more information about the excellent academic programs offered by Kennedy Middle School, or to learn how you can become involved in supporting this wonderful student body, please contact the school office at 555-1234.

Other material, such as brochures, can also be created and distributed to the community. These should be made available to prospective students and their families. This material can be used to promote the various positive aspects of the school, including the impressive or encouraging results of test scores.

Regardless of the route you choose, it is important that you publicize both actual test score successes and the improvements achieved by the school as the result of the efforts of your teaching staff and students. There is little that will boost the morale of your faculty more than having the principal advertise the excellent job that teachers and students are doing to raise test scores—regardless of how the school and its scores are portrayed by the media.

Getting Parents Involved

The public relations activities stated above are also critical in helping to get parents to buy into the overall school program. When parents understand the real success of your school—versus what they may read about in the papers—the more they will be a supportive, positive force in your local school community, and—more important—the more they will become a factor in raising your student test scores even higher.

◎ **Parents are partners.** Part of the success of having parents involved is derived from viewing and treating them as partners in the educational growth of their children. Parental support is a critical factor in student success.

Throughout the school's testing program, parents can and should get involved in actively creating a positive atmosphere. For example, parents can work on many of the motivational ideas presented in "Issues of Relevance" (page 52). Schools that have on-campus parent centers may consider letting parents develop and lead many of these programs.

Slogans and graphics designed to motivate students to succeed at testing can also be directed at parents. It is important for parents to understand and accept their responsibility in their children's educational lives. Without their support and assistance, the school's test scores cannot reach the levels that are realistically attainable.

The following graphic can help the parents understand the importance of their role in the testing process:

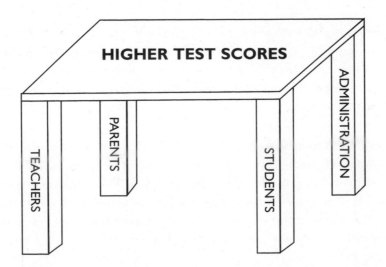

The message of the graphic: each leg of the table is equally strong, and each is equally necessary to support the weight of the tabletop of achieving higher test scores.

◎ **Parent tips for improving their child's test scores.** Even if parents are willing to buy into the school's program for improving test scores, they may not know what to do at home in order to help their child. It is therefore incumbent upon the administration to educate parents in the various ways that they can support the school program and help improve their own child's ability to achieve during the testing period.

Here are a number of very basic tips that are addressed to, and should be shared with, school parents the week before the standardized testing period begins:

- **Make sure your child eats a good breakfast every testing day.** Breakfast provides the energy students need to focus on the test. Hungry students cannot concentrate—that is the reason for many of the school breakfast programs around the country. Just as a football player would not think of performing in a game without having eaten earlier in the day, neither can students work at their peak without the nutritional energy supplied by a good breakfast.

    At the same time, sugar intake should be severely limited at breakfast. This is not to say that a small amount of sugar is not acceptable—but a combination of foods such as sugared cereals, sugared juices, and donuts or cookies is not a good idea. The resulting "sugar high" that is experienced after eating such foods is normally followed by an even greater drop in energy levels, and this drop would most likely hit during the mid-morning testing session. Instead of sugar-based breakfast foods, children should be fed whole-wheat breads, fruit, and some form of meat. These foods will give students the long-term energy they need to do well on a test.

- **Have your child get a good night's sleep before a testing day.** Sleep is as important a factor as a good breakfast. Although children might resist, it's important for parents to insist on a good night's sleep in order for the child to be fully cognizant for the next day's testing. Many students—especially those in secondary school—do not fully wake up until the second or third period. During testing days, grogginess may cause them to do poorly on half of the test, since tests usually begin the first thing in the morning.

- **Get your child to school on time.** Occasionally parents run late in getting their children to school. It is critical that tardiness is kept to a minimum during the testing period. Not only does being tardy create stress in a child, but students who arrive after the beginning of a test are not allowed to join in and catch up. They typically must go to a separate room to wait out the period, then take a make-up exam at a later date. This not only takes the student out of the normal testing environment, but it also causes the student to miss classes because of having to be pulled out for make-up testing.

- **Try to limit morning stress.** Although this may at times be difficult, it's important to try to limit stressful events such as arguments and reprimands in the morning. Stressed students may find it difficult to focus on the test at hand. Instead, they will be occupied with the disturbances of the morning. If at all possible, wait until after school or that evening to discuss problems that transpired that morning.

- **Provide incentives.** Just as the school undertakes motivational programs to get students to try their best on standardized tests, parents can also provide some sort of daily or weekly reward or treat if their child eats a good breakfast, gets a good night's sleep, and cooperates in getting to school on time.

By becoming full partners in the school testing process, parents can greatly assist in raising students' test scores and helping their children reach their highest potential.

Concluding Thoughts

Probably more than teachers, principals face tremendous pressure to raise their school's test scores. Too often the state and local media report scores in terms of percentiles, which rank schools in comparison to other schools in the district or state, rather than showing the real improvements that may have been made to test scores. Raw scores are a much better tool to use to show actual improvement. As an administrator, it's your job to put the scores into their proper perspective and use positive public relations to both promote the real achievements of the school and acknowledge your staff's efforts. Finally, it is incumbent upon the administration to get the parents involved as full partners in the endeavor to raise student test scores.

Creating a Positive Teaching Staff

Grades K–12

Time Line
Address this issue at the beginning of the year when discussing test data, the month before testing, and throughout the testing period.

The Issue

How can I keep up the morale of my teachers and create a positive teaching staff during testing so that poor morale doesn't affect students?

The Idea

Numerous studies have shown that teacher morale and job satisfaction—both positive and negative—directly affects student achievement (Black 2001, Green 2000). This is an increasingly important variable for administrators: if your teachers are not happy, or if they find themselves actually depressed during the testing period, it is quite difficult for them to inspire students to be excited about the testing process. And that will negatively affect test scores.

In the business world, it is said that happy employees are productive employees. It is up to the boss to see that morale in the workplace is kept at an elevated level. The same should be true in schools. It follows that the happier the teachers are, the more effort they will put into their work, the more they will positively motivate their students, and ultimately, the higher student achievement will be. It falls upon the principal, as the educational leader of the institution, to take responsibility for maintaining high teacher morale and for promoting and establishing a positive testing environment.

Given the culture of today's schools, this is entirely logical. Teachers are the ones who are in primary contact with students. It is their job to ensure that students are prepared and motivated to succeed on standardized tests. Administrators have the teachers as their primary contact within the school environment. It is the principal's job to provide an in-service for teachers who administer the test. The one too-often overlooked variable is that it is also the job of principals, as the teachers' direct supervisors, to motivate teachers and keep up *their* morale so as to attain the best effort possible in raising the school's test scores. Remember, even the best students require some form of morale boost to continue to do their best work. So do teachers—even the best, most experienced ones.

As simplistic as this appears, the following graphically represents this critical motivational flow pattern of the school environment hierarchy:

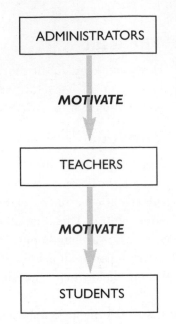

Whereas you are somewhat limited in what you can do to raise staff morale—obviously, the test cannot be canceled, nor can alcohol be distributed—a number of small things can be implemented that will have a direct, positive effect on the attitudes of your teachers.

Acknowledging Teachers' Perspectives

Many things have changed in education in the past ten to fifteen years. Standardized testing and the reporting of test scores have taken on tremendous importance; new types of accountability that involve both the local community and those on the national level have been instituted; the economy has swung in a couple of different directions, often resulting in fewer teacher raises and more cuts in teacher health care and other benefits; and, on top of this, student and parent attitudes and behaviors regarding schools have changed for the worse. As a result, the lives and attitudes of classroom teachers are much different from what they were when most principals were last assigned to a classroom.

It is critical that principals acknowledge these changes if they want to get the most out of their staffs during the testing periods. Few teachers today see any benefit that is gained from taking two weeks out of the school year to administer state and national standardized tests, as is currently the case. No longer can principals be effective by simply dictating how things should and will be. Like it or not, the climate of the school has changed drastically over the past decade or so, and if teachers are going to be full working partners in the process, their perspectives, attitudes, and morale will be a significant part of the equation.

◎ **Be human.** It seems that the higher up one progresses in the chain of command in a school district, the greater the emphasis on test scores. On-site administrators are typically directed by their bosses to review, analyze, and improve test scores on a continuous basis. They are required to attend days of workshops and meetings designed to teach them how to examine, plan, and present test score analyses and the implementation of programs for improvement. They are directed to ensure that all of their staff members have seen, understood, and reviewed the testing data, and they must show proof of this at periodic intervals throughout the school year. Often a principal must prove that the staff has analyzed weak areas and made concrete plans for improvement. This proof comes in the form of various documents that are required to be submitted to the district, as well as demonstrations that these weak areas have been addressed as scheduled at faculty meetings.

One of the biggest problems that you face as a principal is that your teaching staff doesn't realize that you are going through any of this.

Teachers want to like their administrators. It makes for a much more pleasant working environment. They want to relate to you on a personal level. They want to feel that they are working *with* you, and not *for* you. To this end, you should be open and honest with them. Let your staff know about the pressure that *principals* are under in regard to test scores—that the burden is not only on teachers' shoulders. When they complain about having to go to yet another after-school meeting to discuss and analyze testing data, you might tell them about the all-day meeting and workshop that *you* had to attend the previous week.

This is not meant to imply that you should complain that you "have it just as bad" as teachers do. The goal is to show teachers that everybody is in the same situation—that nobody enjoys having to go through this entire process, but that everyone, administrators included, must endure it together.

Granted, this advice is totally contrary to what you were taught in your administrative courses. Administrators are instructed to endorse all ideas that trickle down from their superiors as if they were their own. But this presents a dilemma: how can you come across as a human being to staff members while presenting material that teachers (and possibly you as well) may not fully buy into, while still being responsible to your superiors? There's no easy answer—there's often a fine line between what you are required to present and support and what you know your staff will fully accept. The specific solution depends on each individual situation.

◎ **Be honest with your staff.** When test results are hauled out for the fifth time during the school year and are greeted with an audible moan by the staff, you should make them aware that you are required by *your* bosses to review the data again, and that you must show proof of having done so. When teachers understand that you are required to repeatedly review the material—that these are not exercises that you have *chosen* to put staff members through—teachers will be more accepting and cooperative. It's a matter of professional respect. When teachers understand that you are following through on a directive from your own supervisors, they are less likely to believe that you are deliberately wasting their time reviewing data that they have already seen, discussed, and analyzed. Feeling respected goes a long way toward increasing teacher morale.

◎ **Acknowledge teachers' accomplishments and limitations**. It's important to publicly acknowledge that the testing period is stressful and often unpleasant for teachers. Let teachers know that you're aware that teachers face the following:

- Their daily schedules and routines are completely altered during the testing period.
- They feel that they did not get to cover all of the curricular material that they wanted to cover before the exam.
- They discover test questions regarding material that was neither covered in class nor expected to be tested.
- They may be concerned about possible personal repercussions if their students do not do as well on the tests as they should. (The more inexperienced the teacher, the more this is likely the case.)

All of these concerns are, at least to some degree, in the minds of teachers, and all of them can lead to elevated stress levels. A simple acknowledgment of these concerns goes a long way to raise staff morale. Teachers will feel that they are at least understood, and that their feelings and apprehensions are respected.

It is also important for you to openly acknowledge factors that negatively affect test scores and that neither teachers nor administrators have any control over. Such factors may include, but are not limited to:

- a large proportion of English Language Learners who cannot read, much less comprehend, the tests;
- a large proportion of special education students who, because of their learning disabilities, cannot comprehend the tests;
- the scores of a number of the feeder schools to your population are much lower than yours, and the students were not as prepared as you would like them to be (this is especially common at the sixth- and ninth-grade level); or
- one or more grade levels face extenuating circumstances (see page 77) that may negatively affect those grade levels' test scores.

Every school and community has various other potential extenuating circumstances that should be acknowledged when appropriate. This is not to say that teachers have no accountability when it comes to improving their schools' scores. Accountability is very much a subjective issue, and you should address that when and if it becomes an issue with one or more teachers. However, it is also imperative that staff members believe that you are fully aware of extenuating factors that limit both students' and teachers' ability to improve scores. You need to acknowledge that it is not the fault of the teachers that scores are not higher. Again, this is a basic issue of respect, and it has a critical effect on your ability to maintain a positive teaching staff.

Raising Your Staff's Morale

You can do a number of things to create a positive teaching staff that wants to work to its highest potential and make the testing period as successful as possible. Some involve creating and maintaining a school environment that enforces a positive attitude toward the tests. Some involve physical adaptations that you can establish or alter to promote higher teacher morale.

- ◎ **Know your staff.** The most basic respect you can demonstrate to teachers derives from knowing your staff and tailoring your instructions and discussions to them. Just as teachers use different instruction methods with their students, so should you take each teacher's experience, style, skills, and personality into account when presenting material and direction.

Experienced teachers (those who have taught for four or more years), do not require as much direction and explanation regarding the tests and the testing procedures as do inexperienced teachers. They have been through the process numerous times and know how to administer the exam. In these cases, you may need only to discuss any changes that have been instituted and to review any problems that the teacher encountered during the previous testing period. It's unnecessary, and disrespectful, to treat experienced teachers as if they know nothing about the testing procedure.

Inexperienced teachers, however, do require detailed information about, and instructions on conducting, the tests—especially when it comes to areas that are often problematic for teachers who are unfamiliar with the testing procedures.

One idea that addresses the needs of both groups is to have a separate in-service session for new teachers. During this time you should discuss the basics of the test and the testing procedure, and provide tips on how to succeed at the process. This not only meets the needs of the inexperienced teachers, but it also shows respect for the experienced teachers' time and knowledge.

Along the same lines, if your school is a high performer according to the district or state rating system, or if it has demonstrated consistent increases in test scores during the previous few years, there is probably little need to stress the importance of the tests to teachers, nor is it necessary to pressure them to perform at higher levels. With a school such as this, it's obvious that your staff knows what to do and has been doing it. To treat them as if they were in a low-performing school, or as if they were not doing a good job helping the school reach its potential, is disrespectful and sometimes counterproductive.

◎ **Be as positive as possible.** Accentuate the positive when presenting test-score data to your staff. Readily acknowledge what they have been doing well, and put the scores into their proper perspective. Above all, always focus on improvements made to raw scores and not on the percentiles. There is nothing that you or your staff members can do about raising your school's percentile rating—that is a statistic that is totally dependent on the achievement of every school being rated. However, there is a substantial amount that you and your staff can do about raising raw scores—the true measure of student performance. If raw scores have gone up significantly, and especially if you reach your school-based goal, your should celebrate that instead of bemoaning that the scores—and the teachers' efforts—aren't good enough.

This entire issue is one of a psychological nature. In order to raise staff morale and establish a positive atmosphere, you need to make sure teachers know that their hard work is appreciated, even if their efforts may not be totally reflected in the reporting of your school's test data by federal, state, or local media. Otherwise, a culture of failure develops, and teachers gradually develop an attitude of "Who cares?" or "Why bother?" A major problem will develop if teachers feel that their efforts are unappreciated and that their lack of success is due to circumstances beyond their control. They will eventually feel disrespected, and their morale will be greatly diminished.

If test-score data reveals areas that need improvement, you would do well to select one or two to key in on throughout the following year. For example, if spelling scores are low, urge the entire staff to concentrate on spelling throughout all subject areas from the beginning of the school year through the testing period. It's more effective to target one particular area for special improvement than it is to simply say, "We need to raise our overall scores." This will direct everyone's attention toward one aspect of the test and away from the implication that teachers need to do a better job on the test in general.

Your teachers are hardworking, educated professionals. They care deeply about their students and their jobs. They are human, too, with personal needs of satisfaction and respect and pride in the job that they are doing. It is critical that you do not overlook these psychological aspects of raising staff morale.

◎ **Make teachers' lives easier during the testing period.** The testing period is stressful. The entire school environment, from schedules to staff assignments and obligations to the physical set-up of classrooms, is in upheaval during this time. Although many of these variables cannot be altered or avoided, there are many little things that you can do to make teachers' lives a little easier, raise their morale, and help create a positive teaching staff during the testing period. The following are some examples:

- **Allow for planning time.** Teachers often complain that they do not have time to meet with their teaching teams, grade-level peers, or departments to review and discuss various issues regarding the standardized tests. They may want to discuss the material on the test, the testing environment, the students who are involved, or the entire procedure itself. Often when they are provided meeting time, there are strings attached in the form of specific agenda items that they must cover or a limitation on the topics to be discussed. Sometimes they have to contend with the presence of an administrator, which inhibits free discussion. During the few weeks before the test, try to provide teachers some unstructured time with their peers to deal with test-related issues—issues that are of relevance to the teachers, ones that they personally select, not those that are mandated for discussion.

- **Provide extra personal time.** Often teachers have to use some of their time at recess or nutrition breaks to collect or return testing materials. Sometimes the lines are long as materials are signed in. During testing days, teachers greatly appreciate being given an extra ten minutes for recess or nutrition breaks in order to let them fulfill their obligations while, at the same time, enjoying a full break.

- **Provide attendance incentives.** In schools where teacher morale is low, teacher attendance is often lower than normal during the testing period. Unfortunately, this disrupts the entire testing environment. When substitutes have to fill in, staff members need to be moved to administer the test, and students are placed in testing situations with unfamiliar personnel. The higher the absenteeism, the greater the disruption to the process. In addition to providing a more positive school environment, you might consider offering teachers attendance incentives. For example, one middle school administrator contacted a local pie shop and acquired a donation of five pies at the end of the testing period. The names of all of the teachers who had perfect attendance records during the testing period were placed into a box, and five teachers were selected to win a pie. One high school administrator awards class coverages, granting any teacher who has perfect attendance during the testing period one free class period during the following month (the period is covered by an administrator). These modest incentives help the staff put in that slight extra effort to keep their attendance high during the testing period.

- **Feed them.** This seems trivial and insignificant, but you would be surprised how much a simple gift of food raises the morale of your teachers. It is already known that teachers will eat virtually anything that is placed in the teachers' room. Just by offering them donuts or bagels on the first day of testing, or by having cookies or chocolate available in the room where the test materials are distributed and returned, you can greatly raise your staff's morale. Teachers look at this gesture as a sign that you care enough about the staff to put in that little extra effort to do something nice for them.

◎ **Treat teachers as partners throughout the process.** The most respectful thing that you can do with your teaching staff is to treat them as full partners throughout the process. Discussions as to the testing schedule—what days to test, how many hours, which class periods should go on as scheduled—should have active teacher input. This is considerably different from simply handing teachers a completed proposed testing schedule and asking for their input after the fact. Teacher representatives should be involved every step of the way in the actual construction of that plan.

This goes for other aspects of the testing procedure, too. Experienced teachers can be involved in the in-service of new teachers. Student and school goals and motivational programs can be discussed and planned with the involvement of your staff. Teachers, especially those who have been giving standardized tests for many years, have a connection to the classroom and to students that no administrator can have, simply by nature of their jobs. They have a unique perspective to offer on many of these issues.

By including teachers in all aspects of the testing program, you encourage them to buy into and take personal ownership of the program. Not only does this demonstrate your respect for their knowledge, expertise, and efforts, it also raises their morale, establishes a positive teaching staff, and, most important, ensures that teachers give their very best efforts to improve the test scores of your school.

Concluding Thoughts

In order for teachers to do their best work throughout the testing period, they must be motivated and have a positive attitude. It falls upon the administration to motivate the staff, just as it is incumbent on teachers to motivate their students. In order to do this, you must acknowledge teachers' perspectives throughout the testing process. This can be accomplished by demonstrating your own humanity, by being honest with your staff, and by publicly acknowledging their accomplishments and limitations. Principals, especially, need to tailor in-service work and discussions to each teacher's experience, personality, and style. You should be as positive as possible, and try to help make teachers' lives a little easier during the testing period by allowing for peer planning time, by providing some extra personal time every test day, by establishing teacher attendance incentives, and, believe it or not, by feeding them. It is critical that teachers believe they are treated as partners every step of the way. All of these measures will go a long way toward creating a positive teaching staff and improving test scores.

Creating a Productive Testing Environment and Administering the Test

Grades K–12

Time Line
Address this issue the month before and throughout the testing period.

The Issue

How can I set up the testing environment and establish a system for administering the tests that gets the most out of teachers and students?

The Idea

Two major issues are addressed here: the administering of the standardized tests themselves, and the establishment of the overall testing environment. The actual implementation of testing procedures is the direct responsibility of the principal and other on-site administrators. Even if a testing chairperson has been named among the teachers or counseling staff, the responsibility for making, and the accountability that comes with making, those decisions, falls directly on the principal. It may seem a simple task to administer the standardized tests, but there are tremendous repercussions connected with the decisions that are made. Many of these decisions have a direct effect on test scores, regardless of any motivational programs that may be in place to raise achievement on these exams.

Some aspects of test administration are commonly addressed in the same way by all schools. For example, virtually every school attempts to ensure that the physical layout and environment of each classroom (such as the placement of tables and chairs and the assurance of a quiet atmosphere) is conducive to test taking. When the testing schedule allows for some flexibility, many schools establish a policy of not assigning sections of the test at times when student concentration is at a minimum, such as on Mondays or Fridays or during the afternoon.

Many other variables, however, are often not considered when administering the exams. These variables can have a significant, direct effect on your students' performance and test scores.

Testing Assignments

In secondary schools, where students travel from teacher to teacher, the problem of determining testing assignments is much more significant than it is in elementary schools, where the classes are self-contained and the everyday teacher is the one giving the test. In both middle schools and high schools, the actual testing assignments are too often overlooked or simply ignored by administrators. Unfortunately, these assignments have a direct influence on how well students do, and their effect can supersede those of many of the positive programs and ideas that you and your staff have implemented to raise test scores.

◎ **Problems associated with testing assignments.** Decisions on testing assignments within the school—which teachers will test which students, and who will be assigned out-of-classroom roles—are typically made out of convenience. As a result of the extraordinary amount of paperwork involved with administering the test, decisions regarding assignments are usually based on the easiest way to keep track of the students and the tests, or on whichever method will save hours of sorting, filing, and packing answer sheets and other materials.

Typically, tests are administered by either the homeroom teacher, who tests his or her students in all of the subject areas, or by the first-period (or second-period, if attached to a nutrition period) teacher, who tests his or her students in all of the subject areas. Those teachers that do not have homerooms or who have a first-period (or second-period) conference act as rovers or floaters (relieving teachers who need a break or who have questions), or as substitutes for a teacher who is absent.

Although, on the surface, this seems a quite logical way to handle testing assignments, there are two very important repercussions of this arrangement:

- Some of the most experienced (and best) teachers do not have homerooms and are therefore not assigned students. This group often includes department heads, coordinators, and union representatives.
- Teachers whose subjects are nonacademic (such as physical education) and who therefore have little or no experience in giving academic tests in a testing atmosphere are often responsible for administering the tests. (This is not to say that these teachers are incapable of correctly and efficiently giving the tests. However, the majority of them have little experience in this area, and for that reason alone, they may not do as good a job as teachers who are accustomed to giving tests that are similar to the standardized tests. Ultimately, why would any school want to take this risk when the stakes are so high?)

Hours upon hours are spent, and extraordinary teacher and administration effort is devoted to, working on strategies designed to raise standardized test scores—only to have those strategies fail because some of the most important decisions that directly affect all of these efforts are made simply on the basis of clerical convenience. This just does not make sense.

◎ **Who should, and who should not, test students.** There is another highly subjective variable in this equation with which the principal must deal. It is common knowledge to those on-site that some teachers do very well in testing situations with their students, and some teachers do poorly. This becomes a matter of accountability for the administration. Teachers who perform poorly at giving tests remain on a school's staff for many reasons, from having strengths in other areas that make them valuable assets to being contractually protected from removal. Nevertheless, administrators are well aware that some teachers simply should not be allowed to administer the standardized tests to students. This is an extremely important variable when one considers the following equation, which holistically encompasses the entire testing preparation and environment of the school:

> Well-Qualified, Motivated Teachers +
> Well-Prepared, Motivated Students +
> A Positive Testing Environment Created by the Administration =
> Higher Test Scores for the School

The decision on whether or not to allow any particular teacher to administer the test to students must be based on your knowledge of that teacher. Just as teachers know the strengths and weaknesses of their students, so should you know the strengths and weaknesses of your teachers. Although the decision is highly subjective, it is one that you, as the leader of your school and as the person who is ultimately held accountable for test scores, are qualified to make.

Consider the following true story. One year, an urban middle school's test scores were presented in such a way that showed how each specific testing group—the homeroom—had performed the previous year. Not only did the homeroom stay together, but the recording sheets also included information on how well students did on the standardized testing the previous year as a comparison. The results were quite shocking. In a number of homerooms in which teachers of nonacademic subjects administered the tests, the *majority* of students' scores significantly fell. At the same time, the scores of students in some of the homerooms taught by experienced teachers of academic subjects rose *across the board*.

The implications of this analysis were tremendous. Despite all of the hard work of the staff and the students to prepare for the various exams, ultimately, student achievement hinged largely on who administered the tests.

The worst part of the story is that when the data was presented to the administration, it was determined that the same homeroom teachers would continue to give the test because, from a clerical standpoint, it was more convenient to administer it during homeroom. That is the type of decision that not only hurts the school, but destroys the morale of those on staff who have worked so hard to help raise scores.

Ultimately, teachers of academic subjects have more experience in giving exams and in ensuring a good testing environment. When they are testing their own students, they know who to watch out for, where problems may arise, and how to solve those problems quickly and efficiently without disrupting others in the room. For the most part, teachers of nonacademic subjects normally see the same students in a completely different environment—often one in which behaviors vary from the silent, highly structured environment of standardized test taking.

Obviously, there are exceptions, and those exceptions should be taken into account. Many teachers of nonacademic subjects have taught academic subjects in the past, or happen to excel in a testing environment. These teachers should absolutely administer the test. Similarly, there are a number of teachers of academic subjects who either have poor classroom management skills (and who therefore do a poor job of controlling students during testing) or simply have a negative view of the test or consider it irrelevant (and therefore put less-than-adequate effort into the administration of the exams). Under no circumstances should these teachers be administering these critical standardized tests. You should know which of your teachers fit into each category.

In order to maximize students' potential, it is imperative that you select only those teachers who excel at administering tests to participate in the administration of the standardized tests. You can still have the majority of homeroom or first-period teachers give the exam, just replace those whom you feel need to be replaced. This ensures that most of the teachers whose subjects are academic, regardless of whether or not they have homerooms or first-period classes, would be selected to administer the exam. Teachers of nonacademic subjects who have demonstrated excellence in the standardized testing environment should also be selected to administer the exam. The remaining teachers should be rovers or substitutes.

Some of these changes may result in the unhappiness of some teachers—and yes, that unhappiness will affect staff morale to some extent. However, as the saying goes, you can't make everyone happy all of the time. And in this situation, the stakes are simply too high. Too much effort has gone into improving test scores to ruin it by having the wrong people administer the test. You may also be pleasantly surprised—many of the academic teachers will be delighted that they are allowed to give the test, and many of those teachers who are designated as rovers will be equally happy.

Establishing a Successful Schoolwide Testing Climate

The principal of a school is comparable to the CEO of a large corporation. Just as the CEO is ultimately responsible for the overall climate of his or her corporation, you are ultimately responsible for the overall climate of your school. Regardless of how much or how little you are directly involved in establishing a positive, successful testing program and environment, it is you, the principal, who are ultimately held accountable for that program.

Throughout this book, a number of issues that relate to standardized testing have been discussed. The following is a review of these issues from the administration's perspective. Besides the actual administration of the exams, all of these other variables need to be addressed in some fashion if you want to have your school reach its potential and achieve the highest score that it can on the standardized tests. Whether you handle these areas of concern personally, delegate them to other administrators, or whether the teachers themselves fulfill the obligations, you need to ensure that these areas are all adequately addressed.

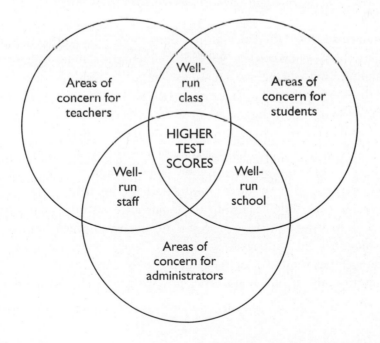

◉ **Areas of concern for teachers.** Probably the greatest area of concern for your teachers is the problem they face trying to ensure that all material to be tested is included in the classroom curricula while simultaneously maintaining their personal teaching independence. Advance planning is critical when dealing with this situation. Teachers need to develop personal pacing plans and prioritize concepts and standards to be taught. It also helps them if they integrate curricular material whenever possible, both within a subject area and across subject areas. This is especially important when teachers are required to implement district pacing plans, benchmark assessments, and prescribed programs. Providing teachers with extra time can greatly assist with this preparation.

Sometimes teachers find that material found on the final standardized exam is not included in the class textbook. This is especially the case when either the test or the textbook are designed for nationwide use and are not aligned with state standards. In this situation, it is important for teachers to analyze the textbooks and determine what material is inadequately covered or completely missing from the book. Teachers can then incorporate the teaching of this material into their personal pacing plans. The Internet can serve as the ultimate teaching resource center to provide this material. With the acquisition of digital literacy, both general education Web sites and comprehensive subject-matter Web sites can quickly and efficiently lead them to free, excellent curricular material. You can assist teachers in these endeavors by giving them extra prep time and by ensuring that every teacher has access to the Internet within their classroom.

Standardized tests often include questions about subjects that were not covered in class, even when teachers have followed the standards. In order for students to succeed in these situations, it is critical that they develop critical thinking skills so that they can *find* the correct answers on the tests even if they do not *know* the correct answers. Critical thinking skills can be developed in the classroom through the use of careful teacher questioning techniques and through student practice. With careful planning, teachers can teach their students how to think. You can help by supporting teachers with critical-thinking staff development.

It's crucial that students buy into the importance of study and test-taking skills in order to succeed on exams. As much as they may initially resist, students need to internalize the value of learning and practicing these skills if they want to do better and raise their scores. Students need to learn how to study effectively and efficiently, with an emphasis on the *quality*, not the quantity, of study hours. They need to learn test-taking strategies so they can locate the correct answers on tests even when they don't know that particular material. Finally, they need to view their study habits holistically, taking into account both their study environment and their physical states. These are all study and test-taking skills that need to be taught by the classroom teachers. By taking all of these aspects into account, students have a greater chance of succeeding on tests. Sharing this type of information with parents on a schoolwide basis would support these teacher efforts.

Teacher morale directly affects student achievement. This is especially the case during the testing period. It is important for the teachers themselves to try to improve both their own and their peers' morale. However, you can support their efforts by actively promoting the concept of veteran teachers working as mentors for inexperienced teachers. Experienced teachers can share testing tips, review directions and procedures that are unique to the test, and put the test into perspective for new teachers. All teachers can benefit from partnerships with fellow staff members who share the same or similar students. Finally, teachers can reduce stress during the testing period through the use of food, camaraderie, and the daily sharing of jokes.

◎ **Areas of concern for students.** A number of student-related issues must be taken into account in any attempt to raise school test scores. Regardless of all of your plans for raising the scores, unless you have the full cooperation of students themselves, all plans for raising scores will come to naught. Teachers are the primary people in the school who need to motivate students to try to do their best on the exams. This can be accomplished through both extrinsic and intrinsic motivational activities such as attendance incentive programs and "school spirit" programs that establish a positive testing atmosphere. Teachers also need to deal with student stress, which can reduce test scores. By preparing students for the test, teaching relaxation techniques, and putting the test into perspective for students, teachers can help alleviate this problem. Your support of these endeavors is critical. In addition, you need to understand that those who are required to test students with special needs face unique problems. In addition to traditionally testing low, special-needs students must deal with the negative self-esteem that is often produced as the result of being forced to take a test that is normally well above their abilities. You should ensure that IEP directives take precedence over state- or district-specified testing procedures, that special-needs students are taught the skills that are required to take the test, and that these students are mentally prepared for the testing experience.

One of the best ways to help all students improve their ability to learn and to succeed on tests is to work on activating their thinking processes. Multiple intelligences theory can greatly assist teachers in accomplishing this goal. Through the use of this theory, student problems can be diagnosed, and each student's preferred intelligence can be capitalized on in order to help them learn problematic material. Teachers can also manipulate their classrooms to provide a better thinking environment for testing non–verbal-linguistic and non–logical-mathematical students, especially during standardized testing periods. You can expedite this process by providing staff development in the theory of multiple intelligences.

◎ **Areas of concern for administrators.** It seems that the most significant job of administrators today involves dealing with test scores both on site and with parents. Probably more than teachers, you face tremendous pressure to raise your school's test scores. Too often the state and local media present score results in the form of percentiles that rank schools rather than displaying actual individual school improvement. Raw scores are a much better tool to use to show actual improvement. You need to put the scores into their proper perspective and use positive public relations to both promote the real achievements of the school and to acknowledge the staff's efforts. Finally, it is your job to get parents involved as full partners in the endeavor to raise student test scores.

Creating a positive teaching staff is critical in getting teachers to do their best work throughout the testing period. It falls directly upon the administration to motivate the staff, just as it is the responsibility of teachers to motivate their students. You must acknowledge teachers' perspectives throughout the testing process. This can be accomplished by being human, by being honest with the staff, and by publicly acknowledging teachers' accomplishments and limitations. Principals, especially, need to tailor both in-service work and full-staff discussions to the experience, style, and personality of each teacher. You should present as positive an attitude as possible and try to make teachers' lives a little easier during the testing period. You can accomplish this by allowing for peer planning time, providing some extra personal time every test day, establishing teacher attendance incentives, and, believe it or not, feeding them. Throughout the entire process, it is critical that teachers feel as if they have been treated as partners. All of this will go a long way toward creating a positive teaching staff, and ultimately, higher test scores.

Concluding Thoughts

Two of the most important issues you will face as a principal are the administration of the test itself and the establishment of the overall direction of the testing environment. Testing assignments directly affect student scores, often in spite of all other efforts made toward achievement. You should ensure that the right teachers—those with the best histories of giving tests in a highly structured environment—give the standardized tests to students, and you should avoid using those teachers whose classroom management skills are lacking. In addition, you need to look at all of the areas of concern for both teachers and students and do what can be done to support them. It is only by taking a holistic approach to maximizing the efforts of teachers, the administrative staff, and the student body that you can establish a successful schoolwide testing climate—one that ultimately leads to higher test scores for all students.

A Treasure Chest of Teacher Tips

The ideas and concepts presented throughout this book are by far not the final word on the subject. Teachers across the country have been giving tests for years. Many of them have their own styles and ideas, just as you do, that have proved very effective.

The following is a collection of test taking tips used by classroom teachers from all over the United States. They are divided into three categories:

◎ General tips: ideas that are not subject-matter specific and can be used in or adapted for all areas
◎ Language Arts tips: ideas designed especially for language arts classes
◎ Math tips: ideas designed especially for math classes

Because language arts and math are the two most prevalent sections of end-of-year standardized tests, these subjects are given specific emphasis here.

Most of the ideas found in this section can be adapted to some degree for all levels, K–12. It is up to you, as the classroom teacher, to select and adapt the information if necessary to make it relevant for your particular students.

General Tips

"Many of the questions on tests are heavy on content vocabulary, even in the math, social studies, and science sections. Even if the students know the skills required, they may have little familiarity with these terms. This is because we as teachers tend to break down the material and simplify it for them. In my school, we as a department have agreed upon a set of vocabulary words for each chapter. The students look up and define the words, create flash cards, work on a crossword puzzle using the vocabulary (see www.puzzlemaker.com), and finally are tested on the examples provided."

—Edward C.

"The strategy I use with my primary students, who are, of course, new to testing, is to present each classroom test, from the beginning of the year, in a formal testing manner. This includes our weekly spelling tests, our reading program exams, and any math assessments. During all of these tests, we follow formal testing procedures. Each student has their own testing space; no talking is allowed until all of the tests have been collected; and no one is allowed to leave their seats until everyone is finished. The students then become accustomed to testing procedures so that the end-of-the-year standardized testing is considerably less nerve-racking for them."

—SUE P.

"Here are some pointers I share with my students throughout the year, especially before testing periods. I teach them to look beyond just the tests, and that these concepts can not only help them on their exams, but will also assist them in school and in life in general.

- **Goals.** Set some goals for yourself. What do you want to achieve this semester in school? What do you want to achieve on this test or project?
- **Establish a routine.** Set up regular times to do your homework, play, and go to bed. If you don't have any assigned homework one night, read something of interest to you. Watch only as much television as you study, read, do crafts or hobbies, and communicate with family members or friends.
- **Ask for help.** If you don't understand something—ask the "stupid" question, one that prevents you and others from being lost. If you still don't quite get it, talk with the teacher or another person at another time. The old proverb says, "Ask and you will receive," and it works more often than you think.
- **Eat well.** Without the proper fuel, a race car won't go as fast. Similarly, without the right fuel, or food, in you, your whole body will not function at its optimum level. The physical, mental, and spiritual aspects of you will not work as well. Eat fresh, whole, and unadulterated (no additives) food. Eat less—or, even better, no—sugar.
- **Get a buddy or work with a team.** Have a friend who you will see and talk with each day. During some of the time you spend together, support each other's development toward your goals.
- **Be physically active.** At least thirty minutes a day, walk, run, fly a kite, play, skip, swim, or anything else that raises your heartbeat....This activity makes your body healthier, opens energy channels so you feel more energetic, makes your mind work better, and it even helps you to sleep better."

—KURT K.

"I do a number of things to help raise the students' test scores. Besides praying a lot, I involve parents as much as possible. I find that one-on-one attention whenever possible, even for a minute or two, really helps the students. I constantly work on building vocabulary. I focus on getting the students to relax before the test in order to try to reduce their anxiety. Finally, I continually promote self-esteem. If they . . . think they can (even though they can't), they may improvise and get the answers correct."

—JANE O.

"The key to passing a test successfully lies in setting clear and consistent goals, planning and organizing lessons, efficiently using the instructional time, constantly reflecting on practices, and employing a wide variety of teaching and learning strategies. Having this in mind while teaching, I focus on my students' conceptual understanding, critical and analytical thinking skills, and problem-solving activities. I help students to construct knowledge rather than reproduce a series of facts. I provide tools such as problem-solving and inquiry-based learning activities with which students formulate and test their ideas, draw conclusions and inferences, and pool and convey their knowledge in a collaborative learning environment. I pose questions and problems, then guide students to help them find their own answers. By doing this, I transform students from passive recipients of information to active participants in the learning process. Students formulate their own questions (inquiry), conduct whole-group discussions and think aloud. When students review and reflect on their learning processes together, they can pick up strategies and methods from one another. I coach, moderate, and suggest, but allow the students room to experiment, ask questions, and try things that don't work."

—LANA L.

"Vocabulary is a major part of all of the sections of the test, not just for the language arts portion. Throughout the year, I categorize subject-based vocabulary words. The students then define them and are tested on the definitions. For example, in a geography unit, the words are divided up into water terms, land terms, mountain terms, map terms, and map-reading terms. Within each category on the test, I use simple definitions that enable the students to differentiate between similar terms. Through the use of a multiple-choice test, I group similar terms (e.g., sound, gulf, bay, fjord) and provide them the same choices four times in order to help them differentiate and analyze the material."

—GERI B.

"I always post-test the skills for which the students are held accountable on the grade-level standards. Then I analyze the results to see if the students met a mastery level or not. Afterwards, I construct a list of students that need a second dose of instruction, which they get while the others who have already achieved mastery are working on independent activities. I also construct games and activities that provide practice for these students. Finally, it is important to give them lots of empowerment talk to build their confidence whenever they become discouraged."

—MARY W.

Language Arts Tips

"I have found it to be a successful strategy to go beyond the test with language arts. I don't teach to the test, but instead I encourage thinking about literature. We use various literacy devices every day: setting, plot, character, point of view, conflict, and theme. Eventually, they become second nature by the time the students take the standardized tests. We continually work on vocabulary from Latin and Greek roots. Honing writing skills throughout the year also helps the students on their tests. Finally, we review grammar daily. This assists them with writing, and then they think clearly about sentence patterns."

—JEANETTE H.

"I teach a small amount at a time, but I do it every day. For example, my vocabulary lessons are no longer than twenty minutes a day and contain no more than a few words. I use the words in class in everyday conversations and expect the children to do the same. They get rewarded if they use one of our vocabulary words in their speech. To teach writing, I use mini-lessons on hooks, topic sentences and supporting details, effective conclusions, etc. to model and have children practice writing strategies. I model the concepts, we discuss them, then they have a chance to practice either in pairs or individually. I teach writing with the direct instruction approach. This includes mini-steps with good modeling, then time for structures practice, followed by constructive feedback. Take, for example, narratives: day one would be what a narrative is. Day two would be a whole-group brainstorm of topics that might be of interest to us. This would include a pair/share....Then students choose a topic to write about. Day three might be what a hook is and how it helps to entice the reader to read the piece. Models of hooks would be presented, followed by a class discussion and then the creation of hooks by the students themselves. By giving very direct instruction in small pieces helps the students digest the information presented to them."

—AIDA T.

"Many of my students do not know how to read! And I don't mean read as in words. Students are not aware of what is being asked of them, so when they answer questions, the answers are completely wrong and way off track. In order to help them read, my students now have to write out the questions and highlight, underline, and/or circle key words. This same process is completed on their copy of the standards. Next, they look up the word in a dictionary if they do not know or understand the meaning. Hopefully, by going through this process, students will feel more comfortable with using a dictionary, and thus increase their vocabulary knowledge and begin to answer questions correctly. My goal is that eventually my students will not have to write out the questions because they have become visually aware of key words and understand what is being asked. Ultimately, this should result in test questions being answered correctly."

—LINDA W.

"I make up workbook practice booklets for my students. These are for them to advance their fluency. They are then sent home for nightly work with their parents. I also have the students work in pairs and time each other on their reading. Buddy reading between grade levels also helps. In my homework packet two weeks before the test, I include test-taking tips for both students and parents, such as getting them to school on time, eat breakfast, etc."

—CAROLYN A.-M.

Math Tips

"One strategy I use in mathematics is to take cartoons that incorporate math concepts and have the students analyze them and write what is good about them, and what is incorrect. This helps the students develop a critical eye concerning what they read and believe in math."

—TOM G.

"I have found that working in groups during warm-ups helps my pre-algebra students. I randomly select students to go to the board and work the problems. I have never had a student refuse to go to the board because they receive points for their group for going up, along with a trip to the blue box (which contains penny candy). When a student does the problem incorrectly, he selects a student to teach him the correct procedure. After the student has learned how to work the problem, he explains what he has learned to the class. Both teacher and learner receive points and a trip to the blue box. Students have the opportunity to question their peers if they don't understand explanations or answers. Everyone is engaged in learning, and the thinking and analysis skills they use directly relate to better performance on all of my tests."

—VICKIE D.

"Test-taking in math entails some specialized skills which I review with my students. First, they are instructed to go through the test and do all of the questions that they can answer immediately. Then they go back and do the questions they know how to do, but may take some time to complete. If time permits, only then do they go back to the questions that they are not sure about. In any event, at the end, if there is no penalty for guessing, they should guess on the questions for which they have no clue. By going through tests in this fashion, the students will know that they will always get the problems correct that they know how to do, and not miss any due to lack of time for completing the exam."

—ROBERT S.

"I tried teaching traditional test-taking strategies (such as substitute simple values in equations, make a simpler problem, eliminate obvious wrong answers, etc.), but I was dissatisfied with the results. I came to realize that my students were having trouble using intuitive strategies because they didn't understand the language of math—they didn't understand what was being asked. I have students who test well below average. Their difficulty with math is frequently conceptual, so my solution is conceptual. Every day, in every class, I emphasize the language component of math by saying, 'Treat your mathematics study as if you were learning a foreign language. We use math to communicate ideas. No matter what level you are working at, if you learn the meanings of the words and ideas of math, the rules become easier and then the numbers become easier.' I'm happy to say this language-based approach has helped most of my students learn more and do better on tests."

—PATRICK D.

Reference List

Armstrong, T. 2000. *Multiple intelligences in the classroom,* 2nd ed. Alexandria, VA: Association for Supervision and Curriculum Development.

Barker, R. T., G. H. Gilbreath, and W. S. Stone. 1998. The interdisciplinary needs of organizations: Are new employees adequately equipped? *Journal of Management Development* 17(3):219–32.

Black, S. 2001. Morale matters: When teachers feel good about their work, research shows, student achievement rises. *American School Board Journal* 188(1):40–43.

Bloom, B. S., ed. 1956. *Taxonomy of educational objectives, handbook I: Cognitive domain.* New York: David McKay.

Carnevale, A. P. 1991. *America and the new economy.* Research report, ERIC Clearinghouse number CE058361.

———. 1996. Liberal education and the new economy. *Liberal Education* 82(2):4–11.

———. 2002. Preparing for the future. *American School Board Journal* 189(7):26–29, 47.

Education World. September 23, 2004. The weekly survey: How much more stressful has teaching become over the past five years? www.educationworld.com.

Eisner, E. W. 1994. *The educational imagination,* 3rd ed. New York: Macmillan Publishing Co., Inc.

Gardner, H. 1993. *Multiple intelligences: The theory in practice.* New York: Basic Books.

——. 1999. *Intelligence reframed: Multiple intelligences for the 21st century.* New York: Basic Books.

Gilster, P. 1997. A new digital literacy: A conversation with Paul Gilster. *Educational Leadership* 55(3):6–11.

Green, M. Y. 2000. What makes a quality school? *NEA Today* 19(1):28–29.

Hardy, L. 2003. Overburdened, overwhelmed. *American School Board Journal.* 190(4):18–23.

History Alive! 1999. Palo Alto, CA: Teachers' Curriculum Institute.

Jones, E., G. D. Gottfredson, and D. C. Gottfredson. 1997. Success for some: An evaluation of a success for all program. *Evaluation Review* 21(6):643–70.

Mandel, S. 1991. *Responses to cooperative learning processes among elementary-age students.* Doctoral dissertation, ERIC Clearinghouse number ED332808.

——. 2003a. *The new-teacher toolbox: Strategies for a great first year.* Chicago: Zephyr Press.

——. 2003b. *Cooperative work groups: Preparing students for the real world.* Tucson: Corwin Press.

Namioka, L. 1987. The all-American slurp. In D.R. Gallo, ed., *Visions: Nineteen short stories by outstanding writers for young adults.* New York: Delacorte Press.

Pogrow, S. 2001. Avoiding comprehensive schoolwide reform models. *Educational Leadership* 58(8):82–83.

Presseisen, B. Z. 1985. Thinking skills: Meanings, models, materials. In A. L. Costa, ed., *Developing minds: A resource book for teaching thinking.* Alexandria, VA: Association for Supervision and Curriculum Development.

Wayne, F. S. et al. 1992. Vital communication skills and competencies in the workforce of the 1990s. *Journal of Education for Business,* 67(3):141–46.

Index

About the Author

In his over twenty-five years as an educator, Scott Mandel has served as a teacher, an administrator, a curriculum writer, and an in-service leader. Currently he teaches English and history at the Pacoima Middle School Television, Theatre, and Fine Arts Magnet in Los Angeles. He received his Ph.D. in curriculum and instruction from the University of Southern California; his current areas of professional specialization include classroom management, teaching methodologies, new teacher education, and using the Internet in educational settings. A National Board Certified teacher, Scott is the author of nine previous books as well as the founder and developer of Teachers Helping Teachers (www.pacificnet.net/~mandel), a Web site for educators. Teachers Helping Teachers has been offering lesson plans, educational links, and inspiration since 1995.

Also available by Scott Mandel

The New-Teacher Toolbox
Proven Tips and Strategies for a Great First Year

This book of tools for new teachers concentrates on those areas of teaching that normally aren't covered in education courses. Strategies are suggested for handling such problematic situations as figuring grades in a way that is fair and rewards students' progress, conducting parent-teacher conferences, teaching five hours of material in a three-hour time slot, and addressing the needs of special education students in the mainstream classroom. Each problem is introduced through a real-life new-teacher dilemma followed by a statement of the basic issue addressed in the section. A time line pinpoints when in the school year new teachers should focus on certain issues.

Testimonials

This is the book I wish I'd read before my first day in the classroom! How refreshing: an insightful, simple-to-use, reality-based guide of tools to apply and adapt to my situation, and make it a success!

—Karen Glienke, first-year teacher

New teachers should receive this book with their teaching certificates. The entertaining and informative contents are essentials for a smoothly running classroom.

—Jennine Jackson, gifted-students teacher

Gives practical suggestions and would be useful to new teachers of any grade level.

—Christian School Teacher

Paper, 144 pages, 8 x 10
$19.95 (CAN $27.95) 1569761566

Available at your favorite bookstore or by calling (800) 232-2198

Zephyr Press

www.zephyrpress.com
An imprint of Chicago Review Press

Distributed by Independent Publishers Group
www.ipgbook.com

WITHDRAWN

MAY 0 6 2024

DAVID O. McKAY LIBRARY
BYU-IDAHO